Room for Therapy

Room for Therapy

What Helps, Why It Works and How to Start

PARKY H. LAU, PH.D.

Foreword by
Colleen E. Carney, PhD., C.Psych.

Jefferson, North Carolina

ISBN (print) 978-1-4766-5935-0
ISBN (ebook) 979-8-3686-0203-5

Library of Congress Cataloging-in-Publication Data

Library of Congress Control Number 2026026297

Printed in the United States of America

Toplight is an imprint of McFarland & Company, Inc., Publishers

Box 611, Jefferson, North Carolina 28640
www.toplightbooks.com

To Mom, Dad,
and my wife Jessica.

And to my patients—
past, present, and future.

Table of Contents

Foreword

COLLEEN E. CARNEY, PH.D., C.PSYCH.

Room for Therapy is a reflection on the relationship at the heart of therapy. Dr. Parky Lau draws on diverse clinical training across major teaching hospitals and academic institutions, and he synthesizes humanistic psychology, cognitive behavioral therapy, dialectical behavior therapy, and acceptance-based frameworks into a cohesive and deeply human lens. Rather than positioning schools of therapy as competing ideologies, Dr. Lau treats them as complementary languages describing the same essential truth: that suffering is complex, change is difficult, and people are doing the best they can with the tools they have. His early clinical experiences serve as reminders that growth often begins before we feel ready. This willingness to acknowledge uncertainty is one of the book's greatest strengths. It maintains a tone of honesty and trust from beginning to end. Readers are invited into the uncertainty that defines both psychotherapy and life itself. One of the most compelling contributions of this work is its exploration of ambivalence for change, recognizing that all change comes at a cost and improvement can threaten identity, relationships, or a sense of safety. By honoring the cost to change, the book offers readers permission to be conflicted. *Room for Therapy* is for anyone interested in understanding themselves and the therapy process with greater clarity and kindness. The book reminds us of a simple yet profound truth—sometimes, the most meaningful change begins not with answers, but with the willingness to take the next small step.

Colleen E. Carney, Ph.D., C.Psych., is a professor at Toronto Metropolitan University.

Introduction

It was a hot summer's day in July of 2019, and I was a young graduate student starting his first foray into the practice of psychotherapy. I was working at St. Michael's Hospital—a teaching hospital neatly tucked in the heart of downtown Toronto. All students in my clinical psychology program completed their first clinical rotation at St. Michael's as part of an academic-community partnership. My program's training philosophy seemed to believe in trial by fire: I was unceremoniously thrown into the metaphorical deep end of clinical cases. The typical patients referred to St. Michael's were those who desperately struggled with severe mental health concerns. Life had been particularly unkind to these folks. Many of them possessed limited financial means, had minimal social support, and were typically marginalized for various reasons—age, race, ethnicity, and sexual orientation, to name a few. In terms of my (woeful) preparation to untangle these intricately woven problems, I had about one and a half courses' worth of training and a handful of role-play practices in my pocket. Even with excellent oversight from my supervisor, I couldn't help but think that there was a bit of a mismatch in patient complexity and my own clinical ability.

The first patient I ever saw at the hospital was an older gentleman named Mike. Depression had been Mike's close and unwanted companion for the past few decades. Mike struggled with many of the classic symptoms of depression, such as poor appetite, oversleeping, concentration problems, and a loss of pleasure in many of the things that used to give his life vibrancy and color. The backdrop of Mike's life had turned grayscale and he was feeling rather hopeless about the future. Mike had been referred to me to receive cognitive behavioral therapy (CBT), which provides patients with the skills to develop more helpful thought and behavior patterns. CBT is meant to be a fairly short-term treatment with the average treatment duration at St. Michael's being 15 weekly one-hour sessions. Unsurprisingly, this efficient therapy was the treatment of choice within the limited workings of an overburdened healthcare system. However, this fact also meant that Mike and I had about three months to work through 30 years' worth of chronic depression.

Interestingly, the first time I brought Mike into the therapy room, I wasn't particularly nervous despite having little idea of what to say or do with the living, breathing human being in front of me. In graduate school, students often threw around the term "imposter syndrome," which is a sort of self-doubt about the legitimacy of one's ability and whether they really deserved to be in the room. Certainly, having this metaphorical room be filled with internationally recognized researchers and clinicians, some the authors of the treatment manuals that we use in therapy, probably didn't help with this imposter feeling. For me, however, the only time I ever felt imposter syndrome in graduate school was when I would sheepishly nod along while my cohort shared their mutual fears of inadequacy to hide my evidently overinflated ego. Of course, my life outside of academia was a different story. I felt (and still feel) like a perpetual 14-year-old trapped in an adult's body.

To be honest, I didn't consider myself a particularly exceptional student. I figured my ability was about right for my current level of training and education. This perspective can be a bit of a departure from the prototypical overachieving graduate student who is equal parts intelligent, perfectionistic, and neurotic—a fantastic recipe for stellar grades and an accompanying laundry list of accomplishments that make these applicants catnip to admission committees. However, this formula is also a pretty good equation for burnout. Someone once told me, "Graduate school is like a gas. It will take up as much space as you give it." And when perfectionism and neuroticism conspire together to make us scrutinize every word in an essay, memorize the diagnostic manual line by line, and say yes to every opportunity that falls in our lap, the gas known as graduate school takes up as much space as the gas of a lactose intolerant sumo wrestler after demolishing eight heaping servings of mac and cheese.

Weird analogies aside, I did appreciate my relatively laid-back approach to graduate school. Within the therapy room, I would often think to myself—perhaps with the sort of naiveté that only a mildly delusional student therapist could have—that if I just did my best to sit with the person in front of me with an open mind, with compassion toward their suffering and a strong desire to help, that would be a pretty good first step. And I could always run to my supervisor and the treatment manual to figure out subsequent steps.

I'd like to say that my first clinical experience with a real patient was a resounding success and that I was the Mozart of the therapy room, or at least Salieri. In reality, I was the therapist equivalent of Baby Bear's porridge: not too good, not too bad, but just okay. Mike and I didn't fully work through his symptoms of depression during our time together. We managed to obtain evidence that certain valued activities, such as reaching out to a close friend whom he had lost contact with over the years, were helpful in improving his mood. We also reframed some of his initial beliefs that were contributing to a sense of hopelessness. For example, we shifted his belief from "all this work is just a drop in the bucket" to something a little more empowering: "Sure, it may be a drop in the bucket, but with enough drops, we can fill the ocean." Although there were still a lot of drops needed to fill his bucket, Mike was surely in the process of building his own life worth living. At our final session, Mike gave me a handwritten card. Inside the card was a message about how much our time meant to him and how our work together had given him a new lease on life. It was the first and only card I ever received from a patient. I guess I peaked pretty early in my clinical career.

I didn't know it at the time, but my perspective on what makes for good therapy fit well with the principles of humanism. Carl Rogers, one of the founding figures of humanistic psychotherapy, identified three ingredients that he felt were essential to therapeutic progress: accurate empathy, unconditional positive regard, and genuineness. That is, Rogers believed that if the therapist really tried to understand what the patient was feeling and why they felt that way (accurate empathy); that the therapist valued the person in front of them with all their heart for no other reason than for being themselves (unconditional positive regard); and that the therapist was an authentic human being in the room (genuineness), then that was enough. He argued that these ingredients were necessary *and* sufficient. It was the therapy version of sugar, spice, and everything nice.

I thought Carl Rogers had a beautifully human approach to therapy. He viewed patients not as someone needing to be fixed, but rather as someone perfect just as they are. He compared his work with patients to viewing sunsets: You don't ask the sunset to soften its hues or tell it to be slower. You simply watch in amazement as it unfolds.

In some ways, I am still that naive graduate student. I still think that there is enormous worth in a therapist providing space for the patient to be genuinely themselves and affirmed for their struggles as part of the human condition. Some folks are skeptical that having someone listen and validate their experience could serve any truly useful function, and they raise a doubtful eyebrow at the idea that talking to a therapist in this manner would be anything but a waste of time. At the very least, it is certainly not something that they would want to pay for with their hard-earned money.

If we approach humanistic therapy with a little more curiosity, we can find that there is a lot to be gained from these deceptively simple ideas. There is something almost magical about a therapeutic relationship formed through the humanistic lens. Beginning early in life, we learn that other people's love is often conditional. For example, we are accepted when we follow specific rules, meet societal standards, or show interest in hobbies and career paths that are deemed worthy. When we present a side of ourselves that does not match these expectations, we are often met with disapproval. It's like when your mom scolds you for a B- on your history paper or when your dad rolls his eyes and turns his attention back to the TV if you say you want to trade in rugby for robotics. In these moments, we sometimes give up parts of who we want to be in order to appease other people's preferences for who they want us to be. Carl Rogers argued that these sacrifices led to discrepancies between our current self (who we are) and our ideal self (who we want to be). Distress tucks itself neatly in the space between these two versions of our selves.

Because love and acceptance are often conditional, it's no wonder why most people hide their authentic selves and cautiously keep up their guard. A guard, by definition, is meant to protect something. In this case, what is being protected is the feeling of vulnerability associated with sharing our authentic self in fear of rejection. However, if we constantly give up parts of ourselves to satisfy others or to avoid judgment, this can lead to feelings of shame toward ourselves and resentment toward others.

Humanistic therapy helps to close the distance between the current self and the ideal self through cultivating a relationship where a person can freely grow. Research on what makes therapy work consistently finds that a positive therapeutic alliance is one of the strongest predictors of treatment outcomes. A better relationship between the patient and therapist means a better experience with therapy. Indeed, well-known existential psychiatrist Irvin Yalom once said, "It is the relationship that heals."

To highlight this idea, I invite you to imagine being in a place where you can simply be your genuine self, resting assured with certainty that the person in front of you will neither judge nor criticize you. In fact, they will admire you for your authenticity and cherish your vulnerability. It's a sanctuary where you can share your deepest desires and wishes, reveal your inner thoughts, and express your worries and emotions, with each expression being held in the utmost regard. A refuge where you can fail freely, cry unreservedly, and make mistakes and be seen as simply human. A place where, upon speaking on something deeply distressing and slowly moving your gaze up to meet the eyes of the person in front of you, expecting a look of contempt, but seeing compassion and warmth. How relieving would it be when the breath of shameful anticipation that you held in your chest dissipates in a warm hug of empathy? If there was no longer a need to hide from shame or attack in fear of criticism, what kind of person could you become?

It is a beautiful paradox that when we are held in a space that tells us that we are enough that we become courageous to take steps toward becoming the person we were meant to be.

The question, then, is what do people need to fulfill their potential? Abraham Maslow was an American psychologist who was famous for his research on exemplary individuals—Henry David Thoreau, Viktor Frankl, Albert Einstein, to name a few—whom he considered having reached their full potential as human beings. He called this phenomenon self-actualization. In his work, Maslow identified certain requirements that humans need in order to self-actualize. At the fundamental levels, Maslow believed that people required the basic ingredients necessary for survival, such as food, water, and shelter, and they also needed to feel stable in their home and work lives. At higher levels, Maslow identified the need for people to feel accepted in their social circles and valued as individuals. When all these conditions are met, the person becomes more readily able to realize their full potential.

I believe therapy offers a space to meet the human need for belonging and esteem. Each person who comes into therapy is fully accepted for themselves and appreciated for their inherent value. In this case, there are no conditions of worth. There are no eligibility criteria in the fine print that one needs to meet to receive love and respect. And just like the child who feels comfortable exploring the playground, confident in the fact that her parents will be there if needed, the secure base modeled in therapy allows people to take the courageous leap of faith toward becoming their authentic self. It is truly the relationship that heals.

Despite my love for the humanistic perspective and optimism in the human spirit, the clinical training provided in my graduate program emphasized a more skills-based approach. I'm a humanist by nature but a cognitive behavioral therapist by nurture. As I mentioned in my work with Mike, CBT clinicians work on addressing unhelpful thoughts and behaviors that maintain psychological problems. I like to use a short exercise with patients to help them better understand the main principles of CBT. If you're willing, I invite you to participate too.

Imagine that you are walking down the street, and you come across a friend. You smile and wave at them, but they continue walking without acknowledging you. What would be your reaction? What thoughts and emotions come up?

People often have very different reactions in response to this hypothetical scenario. Some folks report that they would feel worried because their friend could be dealing with an emergency. These people express wanting to check up on their friend and see if everything is okay. Others might feel sad because they think that their friend intentionally ignored them; their response is to withdraw. A few might be outraged—"How dare they ignore me! Who do they think they are?"—and promptly take their phone out to block them. And some might just assume that their friend simply didn't notice them and go on about their day. As you can see, people's interpretations can vary greatly to the exact same scenario and the way that we think can significantly influence how we feel and behave. Certain interpretations are also more likely to keep us stuck in a problematic cycle, such as people who consistently interpret situations in negative ways. CBT offers a pathway toward freedom by bringing awareness to these patterns and cultivating more helpful thoughts and effective behaviors to reduce suffering and increase self-efficacy. You'll notice from the words that I use to describe these thoughts and behaviors ("helpful" and "effective") that I am not only interested in validity—i.e., how true the thought is or whether the behavior is "right." Rather, I am also interested in their utility and how our thoughts impact our ability to reach our goals. The reason is that we ultimately don't know if that friend intentionally ignored us, if they were in an emergency situation, or if they simply weren't aware of their surroundings. In that moment, CBT helps us recognize that *any* of our interpretations can be true rather than assuming the worst-case scenario. By offering flexibility in how we think, we reduce the intensity of our distress and give ourselves space to choose our response. Within this choice lies our freedom.

The strategies employed in CBT are quite change-focused. Some folks resonate with the principles of CBT and others don't. In fact, certain individuals can feel invalidated by CBT strategies in situations where it may be completely valid to think, feel, and behave in a certain way. For example, people struggling with chronic pain or having experienced significant trauma may find a therapist telling them to be more active in spite of their pain or to change the way they think about a traumatic event as rather insensitive. Although a skilled therapist can absolutely make CBT work for these situations, the focus on change can still sometimes rub someone the wrong way. It can feel like a therapist is saying, "You have suffered through a lot, but you need to suck it up and change the way that you are thinking about the problem." The "but" minimizes the importance of past experiences that contributed to the person's struggles and their present-moment suffering. This emphasis on change in CBT and the experience of invalidation for some patients is partially what led to the development of acceptance-based therapies. One way that I think about these therapies is that they removed the "but" that's usually implicit in CBT and replaced it with an "and." You are in a truly difficult situation *and* there is something that you can do to move toward your goals. In this case, both truths are fully honored.

My subsequent training during my residency year at the Centre for Addiction and Mental Health, Canada's largest mental health teaching hospital, allowed me to delve into more acceptance-based therapies, such as acceptance and commitment therapy and dialectical behavior therapy. These third-wave therapies are rooted in Eastern philosophies. Their principles emphasize an acceptance of life's pain without excessive struggling. The goal in acceptance-based therapies is therefore not to eliminate pain; rather, it is to ensure that the hurt doesn't stay with us longer than necessary or allow the pain to take us away from the most important things in our lives.

Some people wonder whether there is truly power in acceptance.

I mean, isn't acceptance the same as giving up? The short answer is no. Acceptance and change are not mutually exclusive. In fact, they mutually benefit each other. For example, by accepting our current reality and facing the facts of a situation, we become better able to identify areas for change. This then allows us to cope more effectively with conditions like chronic pain. By accepting that pain might be a constant companion in our life, we can then direct our resources to managing the symptoms and focusing on doing the things that matter most to us. In sleep-related problems, people with insomnia find that white knuckling to force sleep to happen is often a recipe for spending the whole night awake. However, if we let go of our constant striving and accept the possibility that sleep may not come, the insomnia unravels and sleep comes more easily.

An aspect of acceptance-based therapies that I truly find integral to human life itself is the emphasis on values. Values are the lifeblood that gives our lives meaning. I'll discuss values a lot in this book because I believe that identifying our values and committing to them wholeheartedly is fundamental in cultivating a purposeful and fulfilling life. Paraphrasing a quote from Nietzsche, people who have a why can bear almost any how. Said less elegantly, we can rest easy, even with the knowledge that life can sometimes be painful, if each day we are living life doing the things that truly matter to us. Regardless of whether we are rich or poor, tired or well rested, sad or happy—could we really say that we are living a bad life if we were acting in accordance with our values? I certainly don't think so. As Stoic philosopher Marcus Aurelius once said: "Just do the right thing. The rest doesn't matter."

Each of these different therapies—their principles, philosophies, and clinical teachings—have made a lasting impact on my development as a therapist. They form the bedrock for me to better understand each patient's suffering and guide my approach to support them toward their goals. Most folks in the mental health profession also end up on a similar journey and become an "eclectic" therapist, combining different clinical experiences and skills that they have learned to foster their unique identity. There are criticisms of eclecticism because this approach seems to lack theoretical foundation. Moreover, the hodgepodge of different strategies may muddy the waters and reduce the efficacy of treatments. Personally, I love it. I think this approach creates a unique tapestry that is specific to myself in how I approach therapy. I also believe that there is much more overlap between therapies despite how we seem to separate them in research and theory. In a lot of ways, the language might be different, but there is much shared meaning in the underlying principles. Moreover, having an assortment of clinical tools is helpful because not everyone benefits from the same tools. Some patients might require a soft touch to allow them to access their inner wisdom whereas other patients would benefit from concrete skills; others still could benefit from a deeper Freudian exploration into their childhood and how these early lessons are affecting their present lives. I'm happy to go wherever is most helpful for the patient.

An eclectic approach, however, is not an excuse to put the patient through the wringer and absent-mindedly try out a bunch of different strategies. In therapy, I apply something called a *case formulation approach*—a fancy term that asks the question "What is it that maintains this person's problem?" Having a large clinical toolkit doesn't mean I now have a larger kitchen sink to throw at the patient. It just means I can pull different rabbits out of my therapy hat depending on what I hypothesize might be contributing to a person's problem. I won't pretend that every patient has come out of my therapy room fully enlightened. However, I would like to think most of my patients have gotten something out of our time together, whether it was a slight shift in their perspective or a reasonably positive experience in the healthcare system. There are also some patients who have expressed their gratitude and shared that they would not have benefited as much in therapy if it weren't for me being on the other side of the therapy room. I won't lie—these heartfelt remarks definitely play a role in keeping my insecurities at bay on bad days. Upon deeper reflection, though, even the tiny changes I've seen in some patients can still matter a whole lot down the line. It reminds me of the chaos theory metaphor where a butterfly is flapping its wings in

Beijing, and in Central Park, you get sunshine instead of rain. Similarly, it is also possible that the tiny changes that occur in therapy can ripple into profound transformations over the course of someone's life. And I do hope that my efforts have led to some sunshine in my patients' lives.

If you're still with me, you're probably wondering why I've been meandering through this introduction and reflecting on my clinical journey in a stream-of-consciousness monologue. I find this a sort of meta way for you to understand who I am, how I think, what principles inform my practice, and what I consider important when working with patients. In terms of my work, I truly value case formulation, which I consider the thread that I can hold on to in the vast expanse of the unknown which we call therapy. Case formulation keeps me aware of the unique human in front of me and reminds me to always be thinking about what maintains the patient's suffering. I consider myself extremely privileged to be in this profession that emphasizes authenticity, trust, and collaboration, being able to exist in space where I can behold a person's growth unfold right in front of me. I am also very lucky to learn from all the incredible mentors who have shared their wisdom with me in various clinical settings: classrooms, private practices, teaching hospitals, and recently at an academic medical center at Stanford University.

In some ways, I see this focus on case formulation as the point of this book: to answer the question of what it is that people learn in therapy that transforms their perspective and reduces suffering—at least from one therapist's perspective. This book is a collection of key principles, clinical techniques, and philosophical and existential ideas as well as fun quotes, metaphors, and analogies that I have found to have resonated most with patients. I wanted to write a book that was wholly mine based on the lessons cultivated throughout my clinical training and informed by the wonderful patients that I have had the privilege to work with during my time in the profession. Given the innumerable books on therapy and self-help, I believe this method of blending scientific research and theory with my own personal clinical work is the best way for me to provide unique value to you. I'll also include stories of my work with patients to provide context to these lessons. To protect the privacy of these individuals, certain information will be modified, but the underlying lessons will remain the same. I'll continue to use the term *patient* in this book, which in Latin translates into "suffer" or "bear." This suffering, however, does not discount the active efforts that these courageous folks have taken to improve their condition by stepping into the unknown of therapy with me. I think of therapy as a collaborative waltz between the therapist and patient where we are both leading the dance. I know a little about mental health and the patient is the expert on themselves. Both are key ingredients for treatment success.

The principles and techniques discussed in the chapters ahead are meant to be flexibly incorporated in your life. Like Bruce Lee once said, we need to be like water. And just like water, I encourage you to stay adaptable and centered within your own wisdom to figure out which strategies are most helpful to you and what principles are most consistent with your values. This book is not meant to give you the philosopher's stone to solve all of life's struggles. I'm not sure if there's something like that out there. If there is, I certainly don't have it. Rather, the ideas discussed are meant to provide a framework for you to flexibly navigate the world based on what I have found to be most helpful for my patients. I recognize that this may be of less interest for some people who were hoping for a clearer answer to life's mystery. I understand that uncertainty can be hard to tolerate. However, I also see so much beauty in flowing through uncertainty like water; in leaping into the ever-changing universe, where everything is constantly in flux and joining the dance of life; and in finding enjoyment filling in the shades of gray between the black and the white. This book is meant to help reframe your perspective and look at life in different ways, to make sense of the past and immerse yourself in the present, and to provide helpful skills to move you closer to the goals most aligned with your values.

There may be concerns about whether these lessons learned in therapy that have worked with other patients will have any impact on your life. To be honest, I don't know. The strategies discussed are grounded in scientific evidence but not even science can say whether a specific therapeutic strategy will definitely work for a specific person. Statistics focus on general trends rather than the individual. However, I have chosen key lessons that I believe are relevant to most people's lives in one way, shape, or form, and I invite you to stay curious about how these teachings might be applicable to your own life.

Finally, I don't think there needs to be one right answer to a problem. Our lives are nested within a larger system that has innumerable moving parts. Any small change to the nuts and bolts of this larger system can have far-reaching effects on our lives. For example, we might think of an emotion as one singular event. You feel sad, happy, or afraid. In reality, there are a number of parts that make up an emotion. We have the event that triggered the emotion, our interpretation of the event, past situations or recent stressors that made us more vulnerable to present stressors, and the physiological sensations we feel in our body. Change one and the whole system changes with it. That's why case formulation can be such an incredible approach to therapy. It's about tinkering with small parts of the system and observing its dramatic impact on a person's life—kind of like removing a Jenga block and watching the whole tower topple over (in a good way). There is not necessarily only one true formulation either. We can make progress through a number of different pathways as long as we are willing to stay curious and experiment. This idea suggests there is no right path toward growth. Reframed in a slightly more positive way, this means that any path can be the right path. And I find it freeing to know that we can't go wrong, so long as we are tapping into our inner wisdom.

Now that we can rest assured with the knowledge that there is no wrong path, let's go on a journey.

1

The Courage to Change

"Bran thought about it. 'Can a man still be brave if he's afraid?' 'That's the only time a man can be brave,' his father told him."—A Song of Ice and Fire, by George R.R. Martin

During my residency year, I was working at an outpatient clinic for folks seeking treatment for borderline personality disorder (BPD). BPD tends to be an uncomfortable diagnosis and there are folks who consider the disorder to be scary and irrational. However, I believe that the essence of BPD can be distilled into the simple concept of stability. People who struggle with BPD find difficulty establishing balance in their lives; they feel constantly pulled toward extremes. They may be completely in love or feel intensely rejected; be on cloud nine or in the depths of despair; and feel either absolutely everything, everywhere, all at once, or be fully dissociated from themselves and their surroundings. All at the same time. The result of these painful and disorienting experiences is an overall sense of instability in different areas in their lives, such as relationships, work, schooling, as well as their sense of self.

BPD is unfortunately rife with misinformation and stigma. For example, there are misconceptions of BPD as being an untreatable condition or that people diagnosed with the disorder are just seeking attention. Neither is true. In fact, scientific evidence suggests that symptoms of BPD can be significantly improved through psychotherapy, with dialectical behavior therapy (DBT) being the gold standard treatment. DBT was developed by Marsha Linehan, who is an American psychologist that started her career working with patients who were highly suicidal and did not respond well to regular therapy. Besides developing DBT, Linehan theorized a way of understanding how BPD is developed through the biosocial theory. This theory proposes that BPD develops from an interaction between biology and social upbringing. Biologically, there are some individuals who are born with a particularly sensitive system for feeling emotions. On a scale of one to ten, emotions—happiness, sadness, fear, frustration—are all dialed up to an eleven. This exquisitely sensitive emotion network makes people with BPD feel like they are braving the bitter Arctic winter without clothes or skin. These intense emotional experiences also impact their interactions with other people. Folks with BPD experience constant invalidation in their social interactions, that what they are feeling does not make sense. It's not uncommon to hear other people say that they shouldn't feel a certain way or their emotional response is an overreaction. Over time, the constant stream of invalidation renders a person unable to trust their own feelings and they lose touch with their inner wisdom. If we cannot determine whether our emotions are appropriate for the situation, then we cannot manage them effectively.

Although it would be easy to slap on a label stating that BPD and everything that comes with the disorder as a terrible affliction, I would argue that this innate sensitivity to emotions is not inherently a bad thing. In fact, I would go as far as to say that this sensitivity can be a strength. It is why many people with BPD are incredibly kind and empathetic. They understand the pain of being misunderstood and rejected. However, the problem is that the constant invalidation has made managing intense emotions extremely difficult. They were never taught the skills to effectively deal with them. If you have ever felt furious or miserable, you will know that it is hard to stay mindful and be effective in those moments. The emotions simply overwhelm the "rational" parts of ourselves. In some cases, these painful emotions pull for behaviors to get away from the aversive experience, such as binge eating, substance use, self-harm, and suicide. Although these behaviors are effective in relieving suffering in the short-term, they can contribute to longer-term issues and keep folks feeling stuck and hopeless.

Because I believe instability to be the essence of BPD, I see the role of therapists to support the patient toward the centered wisdom that exists between extreme polarities. For example, therapists work with patients to better tolerate and manage emotions when the emotions are too intense. For those who struggle with powerful emotions, teachings might include breathing exercises or splashing our face in cold water to activate the systems in our body responsible for relaxing our nerves (a simple strategy but enormously helpful). In contrast, the same therapist may help other patients in feeling their emotions more if they tend to keep everything bottled up. In cases where patients are overregulated and always place their emotions under tight supervision, then having the person sit with uncomfortable emotions is important even if having these feelings suck. This skillful approach of noticing where we are in the teeter-totter of life helps us settle into the synthesis between the extremes.

The balance between extremes is nicely captured by the term "dialectic" which is a fancy term that states two seemingly opposing ideas can be true at the same time. For example, we can be happy *and* sad that a good friend is going off to pursue their dream job. We are happy because the friend is going off to do amazing things. We are also sad because this means we will be spending less time together. In this case, happiness and sadness coexist simultaneously. Understanding the concept of dialectics allows us to accept complicated experiences and make sense of the world in less black and white terms, and to find the grain of truth even in the most extreme positions.

In the same vein, DBT is about balancing acceptance and change to become more skillful in working through life's challenges. The core principle of this idea can be found in the Serenity Prayer: *Grant me the serenity to accept what I cannot change, the courage to change the things I can, and the wisdom to know the difference.* Again, acceptance and change work in harmony and mutually reinforce each other. Accepting the truth and facing the facts of reality—even if it is painful as hell—gives us the freedom to focus on changing what is within our control. Providing some much-needed validation toward our own suffering can provide respite against self-criticism and better allocate our resources to fight for our own life worth living. On the other side of the relationship, working toward change and moving toward our goal helps us develop a sense of self-efficacy. Knowing what is within our limits to control allows us to better accept what is out of our hands. Acceptance and change work with each other, not against each other.

Through the skills cultivated in DBT, our biology does not have to be our destiny. However, in the spirit of dialectics, it's also important to honor how our qualities and traits might serve us rather than outright rejecting them completely. I continue to maintain that there is no such thing as a truly negative trait. For example, I have always been a bit more on the socially anxious side. During my freshman year in college, I was definitely what someone might call a bit of an awkward penguin. I recall being a few minutes late to my first class for an introductory political science course. I took one look at the sea of students already seated in the filled-out auditorium, imagined myself trying to find a spot while hundreds of eyes followed me as I puttered around, and decided to waddle straight home. I also distinctly recall skipping a presentation for my French class because I was too afraid to speak in front of other people, especially in a foreign language. As a result, I kissed goodbye to a quarter of my grade, which upon brief reflection, was an even dumber idea. Needless to say, social anxiety has played saboteur for much of my academics and relationships. It would certainly be easy to raise my fists up into the air in anger and curse my awkward self.

However, this concern about social situations has not been without its benefits. The same anxiety that makes me awkwardly slide out of a packed lecture hall may also be a reason why I'm a halfway decent therapist. I like to think that my social anxiety has made me a lot more thoughtful in the way that I interact with other people. Perhaps selfishly in fear of negative evaluation, the anxiety makes me try to understand other peoples' perspectives more: How they might feel in different situations, whether an idea will resonate with them, or if they are likely bored out of their minds from my incessant rambling.

I fully accept that there are areas in my life where it would benefit me to be less socially anxious (for example, no more avoiding presentations!). But I also honor that social anxiety has played a role in my strength as a clinician, a teacher, and as a writer. It makes me think twice when writing to ensure that an idea reads clearly and that I am providing the most value to the person on the other side of the message. Just the same, I invite you to think about the traits you don't like about yourself and reflect if it serves you in any way. For example, perhaps you feel like you spend too much time overanalyzing and thinking about worst-case scenarios. On one hand, this might feel exhausting, and you might wish that you were a little more of a carefree, glass-half-full sort of person. On the other hand, this tendency could be one reason why people think of you as dependable when things go south. Of course, honoring the areas where a trait may be beneficial does not mean you give up on changing the ways that a trait might be unhelpful. It just allows you to look at the trait again with greater compassion and figure out its place in your life. The main point I want to impart is that there are always two sides to the same coin, and there's value in honoring both sides.

This fact remains true even when it comes to changing something that seems like a no-brainer. There are often surprising, unexpected costs that exist alongside the obvious benefits. I'll tell you a story about a patient named Avery whom I worked with at the BPD clinic. Avery was a young and intelligent person who had been struggling with a lot of instability in their life. They had been in and out of the emergency room throughout the years due to various suicide attempts. To start getting back on the proverbial horse, Avery came into the clinic with a lot of motivation and willingness to change. They attended all of their treatment sessions and they had a stellar track record for completing the assigned home practices. Avery and I had set a number of goals for our year together, including passing their college classes, reducing alcohol intake, and increasing overall stability in their life. They wanted to feel hopeful about life again. Avery did a terrific job going through the Rocky training montage in therapy. They were setting healthy boundaries in relationships, managing painful feelings so that they could approach situations with courage rather than avoiding them in shame, and learning more effective ways to cope with stress without the use of alcohol. Through their efforts, Avery had a successful first semester in their return to college and had passed all their classes. They also revisited old forgotten hobbies, such as painting and playing the piano, while simultaneously holding down their job and making time for friends. Avery was moving toward their own life worth living.

This impressive progress, however, did not mark the start of a happily-ever-after. At some point during the treatment, Avery and I noticed that they were lapsing back into familiar patterns. Avery started to stay out late at bars and drinking more alcohol, occasionally adding cannabis and cocaine into the mix. They were going to work hungover; they skipped classes and procrastinated on assignments; and they started spending more time in unhealthy relationships. Avery and I were both scratching our heads as to why they seem to be sabotaging their own efforts.

I reached out to my supervisor about this regression, and she told me that this phenomenon was actually quite common. After all, change always comes at a cost. She wondered if Avery might be subconsciously reacting to some of the cons of changing and this might be the reason why the two of us were losing steam. I was a little confused at this unexpected interpretation. I had assumed that there wouldn't be much ambivalence to moving toward one's goals. I mean, who wouldn't want to be more stable, happy, or successful? As I continued to reflect, I began to see this more truth in the statement that change is not always all rainbows and unicorns.

For example, we might consider becoming physically fit to be a desirable outcome. However, getting in shape may also mean needing to wake up early in the morning to crush a chest day rather than the snooze button. It may also mean no more spontaneous midnight McDonald's runs and trading in our Oreo McFlurry for a garden salad. Some folks may find the positive attention from other people as a wonderful surprise. However, other individuals might become somewhat disheartened when they realize how differently people treat you when you are twenty pounds lighter. It can be a sobering experience to realize that love and affection seem conditionally attached to something so superficial. After all, beauty runs skin deep and the substance under the skin is still the same. Of course, for many people the benefits of being fit still outweigh any possible costs. At the same time, it is important to honor that not everything that comes with change is unequivocally positive. Ignoring these costs can come at the price of invalidating one's own experience and contribute to feelings of shame.

With this new knowledge in mind, Avery and I sat in our next session with the question: "What did it mean for them to change?" Through our exploration, Avery identified several costs that came with greater stability in their life. First, stability naturally meant less excitement. They found that instability wasn't inherently negative and sometimes it could be exciting to have an "unstable" life. Avery agreed with Ted Mosby in *How I Met Your Mother* when he said that nothing good happens after 2:00 a.m. However, whether the outcome was good or bad, Avery still found that the consequences of staying late at the bar led to fun stories to share with their friends the next day. Stability paved the way for boredom. And boredom persuaded Avery to head out to the bar, turn their single vodka into a double, and be thirty percent flirtier with the bartender. Although Avery knew that these behaviors weren't particularly helpful toward their long-term goals, they certainly made the night a little more exciting. Another cost to a more stable life was that Avery received less emotional support from their parents. Avery was used to their family's constant invalidation—that what Avery was feeling was not important. The few times Avery's parents were willing to put on their empathy hats would be when Avery was hospitalized for serious mental health challenges. Consequently, Avery learned that support from loved ones would be few and far between, briefly interspersed only when they were in significant distress. Success and stability would therefore threaten Avery's ability to receive love and compassion from their family.

Boredom and loss of emotional support were certainly important factors that made Avery more ambivalent about a stable life. However, there was an even more compelling reason for them to stick with the status quo. For Avery, the possibility of success gave rise to the possibility of failure. From our work together, I knew Avery to be a very competent person. Historically, they had no trouble finding success whenever they looked for it. There were many occasions when things were going well and the forecast of Avery's future was excellent: Clear sunny skies at 70 degrees Fahrenheit. However, Avery noticed that these halcyon days of picture-perfect success were often paired with terrible storms that swept away everything that they had built up. For example, Avery told me that the last time they felt stable in their life, everything came crashing down when they were sexually assaulted during a date. As a result, Avery went from a straight A student surrounded by friends to dealing with the traumatic psychological fallout of the assault. They dropped out of school, lost friendships, and went into financial debt, falling from cloud nine into the emergency room of a psychiatric hospital. Unsurprisingly, Avery felt unsafe during periods of success. They dreaded in anticipation of the other shoe dropping at any moment. And instead of letting life kick them down again, they took destiny into their own hands through self-sabotage. This way failure was expected. Rock bottom is not exactly the ideal destination but at least it was safe and familiar. In some ways, changing was more painful than staying the same.

This discussion with Avery reinforced my budding belief that change always came with costs and that it is important to honor these sacrifices. For Avery, the sacrifices for a life of stability and success were less short-term excitement, loss of support from loved ones, and the pain that comes with potential failure. Avery and I took time to process what it meant to change and grieve for these sacrifices. In the spirit of dialectics, we honored the truth that change meant tolerating the possibility of failure. At the same time, we also highlighted the efforts they had taken to learn the skills that would support them to get back on the proverbial horse. Life is indeed fickle. Sometimes the skies will be clear and sunny. Other times life will move into more turbulent waters. Through this conversation,

Avery was willing to accept everything that came with changing and decided to move forward toward their goals. Because that's what it means to be courageous—to be afraid and to do it anyway.

I invite you to consider for yourself what it would mean to change. What are the costs of changing? Would there be a need to grieve for certain sacrifices? Perhaps changing means losing relationships, shedding parts of your identity, or needing to brave the uncertainty of failure. If the judgmental voice in your head and saying your reason is silly, let's turn a deaf ear to it for now. If it feels meaningful in your heart, then listen to that wisdom within you. Even people who struggle with mental health concerns may find that there is something to be lost in improving their condition. For example, people with generalized anxiety may find it scary to let go of worrying because they feel that the worries serve a protective function. Maybe they are reminded of a time where the extra time spent worrying helped them solve a problem. For people who have battled with lifelong depression, they may find that shedding their depression means losing a significant part of their identity. One of my patients who had been depressed for most of his adult life found it unsettling when his depression had improved. It was a good thing, but it also felt like the foothold under him had collapsed. He wasn't sure who he was without the depression. Of course, having these feelings didn't mean that it was better for him to live with his depression. Not at all. We are simply acknowledging that change can be scary and can come with unexpected costs.

It's okay to grieve for these sacrifices and give yourself permission to feel sad. Some folks tend to see this acceptance as a weakness: "You're weak for wanting to stay the way you are, you're a loser." Perhaps this type of tough love can work for some people. However, I find that self-criticism isn't particularly motivating and instead leads to shame. The problem with shame is that the action urge associated with this emotion is not to face our problems, but rather to hide away. Shame tells us that we are unworthy of love and acceptance. It takes away our agency to become our ideal self.

Instead of playing bad cop with yourself, I encourage you to try on a different uniform and give yourself some compassion. Perhaps you can say to yourself: "It makes sense to be afraid." Self-compassion is not a weakness and it is okay to do it scared. In fact, there is incredible strength underlying the ability to love and accept oneself despite perceived imperfections. It's you acting as your own humanistic therapist and treating yourself with unconditional positive regard. As Carl Rogers once said, "The curious paradox is when I accept myself just as I am, then I can change."

One strategy to disarm our normally disparaging side and tap into the place of compassion is through the "best-friend" technique. This strategy is simple but quite powerful. To practice this skill, think about a recent situation where you were being particularly self-critical and instead ask yourself: "What would I say if it was my dear friend if they were in the same situation?" You might be surprised at the words that come out of your mouth.

I used to work at a women's clinic leading anxiety treatment groups. Many of the patients were new mothers. These women were often incredibly hard on themselves. They were wracked with guilt whenever their baby cried and thought themselves as bad parents each time they made a small mistake. Despite their self-criticisms that would even make Anton Ego's reviews pale in comparison, these patients were able to channel incredible compassion to the other group members struggling with similar problems. Similarly, you might be surprised how gentle you can be when your words are directed not at yourself, but toward someone you love. I encourage you to try out the best-friend technique now. Think about a recent situation where you felt ashamed and speak to yourself using the same compassion as you would have for your loved one. The skill only takes a moment but it can have a profound impact on our well-being. This self-compassion provides space to then allocate the energy that is normally used to berate ourselves and channel it toward something more helpful.

Ultimately, this first chapter is meant to guide you toward the idea that it's okay to be ambivalent about change. Having these concerns doesn't mean that there is something wrong with you and it doesn't mean you should stop working toward your goals. It just means that you honor the truth that comes with change. That change can be scary, uncertain, and hard. And that's okay. If it's truly important to you, then listen to the wise words of Eddard Stark. Courage doesn't mean never being afraid. Courage means continuing to traverse through the path of uncertainty in spite of that fear. Now let's figure out what kind of changes are most aligned with your values and take steps toward your own life worth living.

2

Finding Your Why

"He who has a why can bear almost any how."—Friedrich Nietzsche

Values are essential. They could be considered the lifeblood that makes life pulse with meaning. The most important parts of our lives that keep the glimmer of light in our eyes bright even in the depths of despair. A remarkable example of the power of values is illustrated in the life of Viktor Frankl, who was an Austrian neurologist and Holocaust survivor. During the early stages of World War II, Frankl worked as the head of the neurology department at Rothschild Hospital, one of the few institutions that continued to provide medical services to the Jewish people. In September of 1942, Frankl and the rest of his family, including his wife, were deported into Theresienstadt concentration camp. He and his wife had been married only nine months. Shortly thereafter, they were separated, and Frankl would spend the next three years of his life in various concentration camps, one of which included the infamous Auschwitz.

Frankl would later detail his experience as a Holocaust survivor in his book *Man's Search for Meaning*. Within the book, Frankl outlined the abject misery of daily life in the concentration camp. Captives were forced to slave inhumane hours with little nourishment and reprieve, ravaged by sickness and disease with minimal medical care, and treated as no more—perhaps worse—than cattle. Each individual was stripped away of everything that a human being could possess. From this experience, Frankl was able to answer in mind and body the existential question: "When a person has everything taken away from them, what is left?" In the absence of hope, how do people continue to look forward? "How can they find meaning in life?"

In some individuals that Frankl observed, the answer was they don't. These were the individuals who withered away. Their bodies may not have been buried yet, but their spirit had died long ago. Yet, there were also those who continued to endure the unendurable. For them, there was a glitter in their eyes that could not be stifled even in the darkest dark offered by humanity. There was something of greater substance beyond the surface-level experience; an internal sanctity that provided respite outside the reach of the external environment. For Frankl, he had found meaning in thinking about his wife, Tilly. Her image and the possibility of reuniting with her were the sparks that kept the glitter in his eyes alive. She was his why, so he could bear any how.

The story of Viktor Frankl is one extreme example of how our values support us in impossibly grueling situations. They are our guiding stars when we feel lost and cannot see the light in the never-ending tunnel. From these hard-earned lessons, Frankl would go on to develop logotherapy. Logotherapy emphasizes the search for personal meaning in order to live a worthwhile life and cope with the shared human condition known as suffering. Of course, it is my hope that you do not have to experience the same challenges as Viktor Frankl in order to discover the most important values in your life. Regardless of our circumstances, the lessons remain the same: Understanding what is important to us and aligning our actions with these values are essential to infusing meaning into the tapestry of our lives. When behaviors and values are aligned, we rest assured with the knowledge that no matter how treacherous the road ahead, it is exactly the path we are meant to be walking.

In therapy, one way to elucidate a person's values is through motivational interviewing. The goal of motivational interviewing in therapy is to resolve ambivalence about change. People come into therapy at different stages of readiness to change. To give an example let's take two people who are dealing with substance use problems. Sam is someone who struggles with alcohol and came to therapy fully committed to start tackling his drinking patterns. He sees all the ways that the alcohol use is inconsistent with his values, such as alcohol impacting his job performance and making it harder to keep his temper in check when dealing with his annoying family. Despite the fact that he enjoys the occasional Old Fashioned, Sam finds that the costs of drinking alcohol heavily outweigh the benefits. Sam is someone who has already resolved his ambivalence and is committed to making a change. However, Dean might have come into therapy because his wife threatened to divorce him if he does not control his drinking habit. Despite his wife's ultimatum, Dean doesn't consider his drinking to be problematic and feels that he tolerates his liquor well. Unlike Sam, Dean is unlikely to come into therapy gung-ho about stopping his alcohol use the moment he walks through the door.

Motivational interviewing addresses ambivalence toward change. Typically, what happens is that the therapist and patient collaborate to identify patient values and highlight potential discrepancies of these values with their behaviors. For example, Dean might identify that spending quality time with his wife and kids as important to him. He might also acknowledge instances when he was too hungover to take his boys to soccer practice or that he sometimes spends the evening drinking rather than joining in on family game nights. This could be one opening for the therapist to increase motivation to reduce alcohol use by highlighting discrepancies between values (family) and behaviors (being hungover on the weekend).

In the example above, motivational interviewing may have worked to get Dean a little more committed to therapy. However, it is also possible that Dean may have concluded that his current drinking behaviors are fully aligned with his values. He may have said that he was perfectly in control with his drinking and that it was something he enjoyed. He didn't mind sitting in the therapy room to learn more about how to better communicate with his wife but the drinking would stay. And that's okay. The point of motivational interviewing is not to sneakily nudge someone to change based on the therapists' own biases and values; rather, it is simply to explore the patient's values and figure out whether they are living life consistent with them. Although this perspective may not be the same one held by other therapists, I personally believe that there is no one right way to live life. There's only a right path for *you*. This path might include pursuing higher education, reducing substance use, and becoming more confident—or it might not. I am perfectly content to simply let the conversation unfold and stay curious about the person in front of me, non-judgmentally and with unconditional positive regard (or as much I can as a fellow flawed human being).

Although motivational interviewing was discussed in the context of working with a therapist, there are also self-help strategies to determine whether a behavior is consistent with your values. One tool to explore values is a cost-benefit analysis. In this simple exercise, you write out the pros and cons of changing as well as the pros and cons of staying the same. To make this process systematic, you can fold a piece of paper into four quadrants and put each combination (pros of changing, cons of changing, pros of staying the same, cons of staying the same) into their own quadrant. Once you have carefully considered and written down points for each quadrant, you can take some time to reflect on which action makes the most sense. This decision is based on the reasons you have listed out and the relative importance of those reasons given your values. Afterward, you make a choice with conviction and with full acceptance of its consequences, good and the bad

Identifying values is important to ensure that the goals set in therapy are coming from the patient. From a therapeutic standpoint, psychological distress reduces when a patient's values and behaviors are aligned. In some cases, I have found that simply resolving this ambivalence through highlighting that a patient's behaviors are already consistent with their values can improve their condition even when we don't change anything at all. A great example of this phenomenon occurred with my patient Kate who was coming to me for cognitive behavioral therapy for insomnia. She was having a lot of difficulty falling asleep and she would spend at least an hour or two each night tossing and turning before the sandman finally put her out of her misery. Kate wanted to find ways to fall asleep faster and escape her living nightmare.

I apologize for the slight departure (and I promise this all ties in with my point), but I want to talk a bit about CBT for insomnia because the treatment recommendations can be somewhat counterintuitive. The goal of CBT for insomnia is to target the unhelpful thoughts and behaviors that maintain sleep problems. A primary maintaining factor of chronic insomnia is spending an excessive amount of time in bed. This "casting a wide net approach" makes reasonable sense on paper because people with insomnia are exhausted and have a hard time sleeping through the night. A common statement you might hear from someone with insomnia is: "If it takes me several hours to fall asleep, then I should go to bed earlier and stay in bed in the morning to hopefully get more sleep." Therefore, the person who used to spend eight hours in bed when they didn't have insomnia is suddenly spending ten or eleven hours in bed. Unfortunately, within this intuitive response is where the insomnia insidiously lays its trap. The problem with staying in bed too long is that this behavior reduces our ability to build up an appetite for sleep. An analogy I like to use with patients to drive this idea home is the "pizza dough" analogy. Let's say you're hosting a family get-together and you are in charge of making the pizza for dinner. You bring out your trusty 10-inch pan and the ingredients needed to make your infamous Neapolitan pizza. Halfway into the process, you realize that you only have enough flour to make a 7-inch pizza. Ignoring the voice in your gut, you decide to spread out the dough to have the pizza properly fit into the pan and throw it into the oven. The result was that the pizza came out burned and the areas that should be covered with delicious bread and cheese have been replaced by gaping holes. Similarly in insomnia, a person who might only be sleeping 6 or 7 hours may be spreading that sleep into a 10-hour window. Just like your unfortunate pizza, the sleep becomes much lighter and there are more prolonged awakenings at night. Chronic insomnia is a tricky disorder because our strategies to cope with insomnia make good sense but counterintuitively worsen sleep.

Recognizing excessive time in bed as a maintaining factor of chronic insomnia, clinical psychologist Arthur Spielman developed a strategy which focused on improving sleep quality by reducing how much time people with insomnia spend in bed. This is known as sleep restriction therapy. By bringing how much time we spend in bed closer to how much time we are sleeping, we allocate that time to build up our appetite for sleep and reduce the amount of time we spend in bed awake and feeling frustrated. Another problem that comes with being awake in bed too long can be found in the tale of Pavlov's dog. Ivan Pavlov was a Russian and Soviet experimental physiologist who is well-known for his work on animal learning. Pavlov was conducting research to understand the digestive systems of dogs. When it was time for the dogs to eat, Pavlov would ring a bell as a signal for the dogs that food was ready. Over the course of the experiment, Pavlov came to an unexpected observation. He noticed that even when he rang the bell in the absence of delicious snacks, the dogs would begin to salivate anyway. The reason is because the dogs had created an association between the bell and food. This is the principle of classical conditioning, whereby an initially neutral object (bell) over time becomes paired with something that elicits a natural response (food).

Humans are not so much different than animals when it comes to these basic learning principles. If we spend much of our time awake in bed, the brain will gradually create an association between the bed and wakefulness. If you ever had the experience of going to bed sleepy and then feeling wide awake when your head hits the pillow, kind of like a light switch going off in your mind, then the reason may be conditioned arousal. The goal then is to gradually reassociate the bed with sleep by making sure that the bed is only used for sleep.

Okay, mini detour over, back to the main story. For Kate, the plan was to keep to a more regular routine by setting a consistent bed and wake time and reduce the amount of time she spent in bed closer to how much she was sleeping. Kate was also asked to get out of bed whenever she found herself feeling wide awake to restore the association between the bed and sleep. However, Kate's adherence to the recommendations remained low. She continued to go to bed and get up whenever she felt like it. She would watch TV and read in bed. And she would often take naps during the day. Continuing with the sleep appetite analogy, naps are somewhat of a naughty behavior in insomnia because it is like a sleep snack that takes away some of our appetite for the "dinner" at the end of the night.

Kate and I explored the reasons for her less-than-ideal sleep behaviors, and the conversation naturally flowed into a discussion about values. What I discovered was that Kate wasn't sticking with her sleep patterns out of ignorance to the sleep science nor was she keeping to the status quo as an anxious response to these counter-intuitive strategies. She simply realized that these behaviors, which weren't exactly optimal for her sleep, were consistent with her values. She loved spending time in the morning cozying up with her partner and sleeping in on the weekends. She placed importance in flexibility and going to bed whenever she wanted. And she took naps because she's an adult who deserves to be able to take a nap whenever she damn well pleased. In other words, the recommendations of CBT for insomnia were not consistent with her values of flexibility, comfort, and autonomy.

I appreciated Kate for her honesty. I told her what I always tell patients when I discuss recommendations for treating insomnia—that I am not and will never be the sleep police. And that it was wonderful that her current behaviors were already aligned with her values even if they weren't best practices from a sleep perspective. Kate was willing to sacrifice some sleep optimization for the freedom to choose her own schedule. As a result, her insomnia symptoms reduced anyway. The reason is because insomnia is inherently a subjective disorder with sleep anxiety at its core. In Kate's case, she was no longer worried that there was something wrong with her sleep. She had all the know-how to improve her sleep should her values change in the future, but she was happy with her choices for the moment.

The story of Kate is a fascinating case that nicely illustrates the power of aligning behaviors with values. When we are doing the things that are important to us, suffering reduces. Consequently, I have learned that therapy isn't necessarily about making a change; rather therapy is about giving the patient a choice. The freedom to choose the path most consistent with their values. If you are ever presented with the two roads diverging into a yellow wood, as described in Robert Frost's famous poem, I encourage you to choose the one that aligns best with your values. Because that makes all the difference.

I also invite you to take some time to consider your own values. Make a list and write them down. Values can be about anything: education, family, health, adventure, career, kindness, relationships, or whatever else comes to mind. These are the "Whys" of your life. For me, my values include relationships, learning, providing value to others, and freedom. In my work as a clinical psychologist, I have the privilege of sitting in an intimate space with another human being, working to support them toward their goals through the therapeutic relationship. I am able to collaborate with other scientists in the field to study interesting questions and spend time writing research papers and books. I get to learn from people smarter than me every day. I am also able to choose from a mishmash of possible activities that are meaningful to me, including research, clinical work, writing, consulting, teaching, and mentoring. As you can see, my whys guide what I do and how I do it. In some ways, I could argue that the specific career path does not matter. I could be in healthcare, community work, education, or blue-collar work, and it would still be possible to build a life that properly reflects these values. I recognize that this statement comes from a place of privilege. It's easy to say all these things when I am in a profession that gives me a high level of personal fulfilment and flexibility. However, I'd like to think that no matter what I am doing in life, I could still do my best to look for these North Stars and shift a little closer toward them. To still build meaningful relationships. To still create something of value for other people. To still find ways to learn and grow every day. I hope my mildly delusional optimistic outlook does not invalidate anyone who is feeling stuck in their life path. At the same time, I encourage you to reflect on whether there is any way to incorporate some of your values into your life, even if just a tiny bit.

Working toward our values is a lifelong journey. There is no point at which a person can proclaim that they have satisfied their values of cultivating meaningful relationships or fulfilled their value of education and no longer need to learn anymore. They are guiding principles that are never-ending. This is a good thing because we want something that can give us meaning for the rest of our lives. And although values don't have a finish line, you can create checkpoints through setting goals. For example, if your values are related to education, you might set a goal to obtain a college degree. To support this broader goal, you might also include actionable steps by listing out what you can do on a daily basis. If your values are related to family, then you might make sure to give your mom a call every week or plan for a family Christmas gathering. Again, the whys will guide what you do and how you do them. These daily activities and goals become the steps and checkpoints that move you ever closer toward your distant North Stars. With these behaviors and goals in place, each step in your journey becomes suffused with meaning and purpose. Even if there is occasional strife and suffering along the way, you can rest with the knowledge that this is exactly the path that you are meant to be taking. After all, you are living a life that is fully aligned with your values.

3

Being a Curious Scientist

"All life is an experiment. The more experiments you make the better."—Ralph Waldo Emerson

One of my all-time favorite therapy tools is the behavioral experiment. Our minds are constantly making predictions about what would happen if we experimented with something new. The prediction also tends to be rather negative. This makes evolutionary sense as our brain has evolved to keep us safe. Therefore, we are particularly attuned to dangers associated with uncertain situations. However, these negative predictions tend to wiggle themselves into the room even when the likelihood of something life-threatening happening is pretty low. For example, my mind might expect that if I were to grab a flat white rather than my usual drip coffee, I won't like it; that if I were to make a call for an appointment without rehearsing what I am going to say a dozen times, I'll stutter through the whole conversation; or that if I ask the pretty girl working at the research lab next to mine out for a date, she'll reject me before I finish the question.

The prediction is one thing, but we also assume that the prediction—which obviously have not happened yet in the real world—to be true. The predictions are not treated as thoughts; they are treated as fact. If we assume that the prediction is true, there would be no point trying out a new item on the menu, making an appointment without anxiously preparing in advance, or asking that person out. It won't go well after all. We then stick to the status quo and sigh with relief believing that we just avoided a disastrous outcome.

A behavioral experiment is essentially saying: "Wait a darn second,

I just lived an entire hypothetical scenario in my mind. I actually have no idea what will happen in reality. Let me be a curious scientist and test this prediction." The behavioral experiment is a powerful strategy that allows us to be intrepid explorers of the unknown and jump straight out of the beaten path into a world of possibilities. For myself, I decided to be a curious scientist and ask that girl out anyway to test if my hypothesis (that she would say no) was true. Fortunately, my hypothesis was rejected and she is now my wife.

I think everyone can benefit from a little extra curiosity in their lives and make more experiments. However, the behavioral experiment can be particularly helpful for people with generalized anxiety disorder who have a sort of "allergic reaction" to uncertainty. In fact, some people with generalized anxiety might even prefer to hear the bad news rather than sit with ambiguity. For example, these individuals prefer to know with certainty that they have been rejected from their top choice for college than to stew any longer waiting for the news. Intolerance of uncertainty also manifests itself in behaviors meant to increase certainty. For example, a person may have worries about making mistakes in their emails. As a result, they check their drafts multiple times to increase certainty that there are no spelling or grammatical errors, especially if the receiver's name is Birch or Rick. A person who struggles with uncertainty in unfamiliar social situations might decide to skip the event to avoid all possibility of saying anything offensive or boring. The problem with trying to eliminate uncertainty is that the future is defined by constant change, and by extension, uncertainty. There is never a point where we can be fully sure about the future. I could be hit by lightning at this moment. Though if you're reading this book, then perhaps I am still safe (for now).

Hassan was a patient of mine that I saw in virtual therapy who was struggling with generalized anxiety disorder. In our first therapy session, I spent the first half of the session talking to a black screen because Hassan was too anxious to turn on his camera. He feared that my knowledge of who he was and what he looked like might come back to bite him at some point if he were to ever become famous. As a therapist and custodian of patients' most vulnerable details of their lives, he worried that I might leverage this knowledge one day to ruin his life. Although I thought his concerns were unsubstantiated, I could understand from a probability standpoint that there was a chance, however minimal it might be, that this could happen in theory. However, I didn't think that this arrangement was appropriate clinically nor particularly comfortable for me. I mean, in the same vein, couldn't he potentially ruin my life since he knows what my face looks like?

I brought up the fact that by allowing him to keep his camera off I would be colluding with what his anxiety was saying—that his fears were true, and I am indeed a nefarious person who will sabotage him years down the road. I also told him that it wasn't very fun talking to the void and I already do enough of that teaching at my university. To alleviate his worries about privacy, we went through the limits to confidentiality and discussed instances where a therapist is mandated to make a report. There was technically very little that he could tell me where I would be ethically required to tell someone. In fact, even if he were to have killed a person, I wouldn't be able to report that to anybody because the ethical principles only mandate reporting for *imminent* risk. As morbid as it sounds, the person is already dead so there is no imminent risk. For his concerns about me sharing details of his life, I let him know that I certainly wasn't going to risk an ethical violation to torpedo the life of someone whom I just met twenty minutes ago.

After a little persuasion, Hassan agreed to show himself on video. We joked that this was in some ways a behavioral experiment to tolerate the uncertainty that I might actually be evil and betray his goodwill. We also decided that behavioral experiments would be helpful to make him more comfortable exploring the less traversed routes of his life. Hassan worried about many things and his strategies to increase certainty were costly. For example, he worried that he would make a huge mistake at work if he didn't spend extra hours preparing for his meetings. The excessive preparation led to him falling behind in his duties and receiving feedback from his supervisor about needing to be more efficient. Hassan's intolerance of uncertainty also impacted his social relationships. Hassan worried about sharing good news to his friends and coworkers, such as news about his recent acceptance to graduate studies, because he feared that other people would get jealous and cast an evil eye curse on him. His mind had created so many negative predictions about what could happen in the future that he never lived in the present.

I started with some motivational interviewing by asking Hassan about the potential benefits of tolerating uncertainty like he did today by showing himself on camera. Hassan reasoned that his constant worrying made him less efficient at work, it was harder to build meaningful relationships, and the constant predictions took him away from being able to enjoy the present moment. For him, tolerating uncertainty was a worthwhile goal that would allow him to move toward his values of relationships, work, and being more present in his life.

We started with small behavioral experiments. His first experiment was to prepare just the necessary amount for a work client, rather than spending hours scouring every possible document and considering every possible question that could come up. He predicted that without this preparation, he would not be able to help the client and he wouldn't know the answers to any of their questions. The client would then make a complaint and Hassan would be fired from his job. Surprisingly (mostly to him, not to me), Hassan ended up doing a great job. For a question that he did not know, Hassan simply did some quick research on the fly and found the answer promptly for his client. A second experiment Hassan attempted was to let his coworkers know that he had received an acceptance for graduate school to test his prediction that other people would be jealous of his accomplishments. Again, contrary to his prediction, his coworkers were overjoyed by his good news. Within a few sessions, Hassan felt more comfortable with uncertainty, and he learned that uncertainty is not synonymous with bad. In fact, often the outcome of ambiguous situations was positive. Hassan also felt more confident in dealing with problems that came up in his life. He may not have had the solution prepared well in advance, but he could trust himself to be an effective problem-solver.

Although uncertainty is perhaps most prominent in generalized anxiety disorder, putting too much weight on our brain's predictions can also contribute to other mental health concerns. For example, in depression we might predict that there is no point in spending time with friends because we won't enjoy the experience. In insomnia, there may be predictions that getting out of bed when we can't sleep will lead to us feeling even more awake. These beliefs tend to keep us stuck in a depression or insomnia trap. If we treat these thoughts as fact from the beginning, there would be no point in trying anything different. But if we constantly stick with the status quo, we can't expect a different result.

At this point, you probably have a pretty good idea of how to conduct behavioral experiments. Whether you wish to conduct these experiments formally or informally, in behavioral experiments, we are simply taking the stance of a curious scientist. In a situation, we notice that our mind has made a hypothesis—that is, a prediction about the outcome of an action. Instead of immediately accepting this conclusion, we test the prediction with an experiment and allow the situation to unfold. Like a curious scientist, we dispassionately observe whether the hypothesis is supported or not. Afterward, we then write down the outcome and determine if it was positive, neutral, or negative. We also reflect on lessons we might have learned from this experiment.

There is a reasonable assumption that the goal of behavioral experiments is to show our anxious brain that its negative predictions are rarely supported. Although having uncertain situations turn out positive can be wonderful, there are going to be times where the outcome is indeed exactly what our mind anticipated. However, I think there is a good reason to allow negative predictions to occasionally unfold in reality (and not just because I'm a sadist). The surprising part of behavioral experiments is that whether our prediction is supported or not is less important. The way I think about behavioral experiments is that they are always win-win. Either the negative prediction ends up wrong (win) or that the situation plays out exactly how our anxious brains guessed and we can cope with life's adversity (win). For example, you might predict going to a new coffee shop to study would be a total flop because the internet connection would be weak or there would be too many people to find a place to sit. And maybe you were right. There was a big sign out front that this was a no laptop zone and there was not a single empty seat in sight. Shrugging it off, you decide to leave and go study at your usual spot. It wasn't the preferred experience, but you survived. That's the important lesson. You survived.

Terry was a patient of mine who struggled with panic disorder. In panic disorder, people become overly concerned about symptoms of anxiety, such as heart palpitations, feeling hot and suffocated, or sweating. They worry that these symptoms are a sign of something life-threatening, like a heart attack or an aneurysm. As a result, they would grow fearful any time they experienced these very normal anxiety symptoms, which unfortunately made the anxiety spiral until they culminated into a full-blown panic attack. In Terry's case, he would worry that symptoms of anxiety were actually a sign that he was having a heart attack. His dad had passed a year ago from a heart condition so his worries made a lot of sense. In Terry's case, however, he had visited a physician who gave him and his heart a clean bill of health. Through exposure practice, I got him to sit with his anxiety symptoms by engaging in behaviors that made him sweat and increased his heart rate, such as running in place, spinning around, and sitting while wearing a jacket next to the heater. These practices were initially very uncomfortable, but his relationship with the symptoms began to change as he came to the realization that they were neither harmful nor dangerous. And although it wasn't my direct intention, Terry ended up developing a very resilient frame of mind. He realized that he was unlikely to have a heart attack. But even on the off chance that he was going into cardiac arrest, this experience might actually be a blessing in disguise. He reasoned that surviving a heart attack would give him a new lease on life and motivate him to take better care of his health. That, or he would be dead, and there would no longer be anything to worry about. Terry was obviously joking, but underlying this response was incredible resilience—that no matter what happened, he would be okay. And paradoxically, with that willingness to experience discomfort, his panic attacks disappeared. Although I discussed Terry's work in the context of an exposure practice, I see his resilient perspective as one that can be cultivated through behavioral experiments and being willing to brave uncertainty.

In sum, behavioral experiments help to showcase that (1) uncertainty is not always negative and (2) even when the outcome is negative, that you can deal with life's challenges. I invite you to be a curious scientist in your life and try out a behavioral experiment yourself. Just pick one to start. The experiment does not have to be high stakes either. For one of my patients, he started out his journey of scientific inquiry with trying out a new bubble tea flavor. Similarly, you can try out a new menu item at a restaurant, watch a movie at the theatre by yourself, or send a text message checking up on an old friend from high school. Reframe it into a win-win. Either the experiment goes smoothly or you learned that you could cope with an awkward situation. Be a scientist in your life, test your anxious beliefs, and stay curious. The unbeaten path might be less scary and more fun than you think!

4

Evaluate Thoughts, Test Assumptions, Change Beliefs

"Reality is created by the mind, we can change our reality by changing our mind."—Plato

In therapy, I sometimes show patients a fun flower illustration as an analogy for different types of cognitions. The leaves are the automatic thoughts that spontaneously sprout up in our day. The stem represents the underlying rules and assumptions we hold about how life works. Finally, the roots represent our core beliefs—the lens through which we see ourselves, others, and the world. Aaron Beck, an American psychiatrist regarded as the father of cognitive therapy, identified three types of core beliefs that were common in depression: helplessness, unlovability, and worthlessness. To give an example of these three levels of cognitions in action, let's say a person believes that they are unlovable at their roots. From these core beliefs stem assumptions that there is no point trying to build relationships because people do not like them. When they interact with strangers, this person may sprout automatic thoughts like "they probably think I'm boring" or "I should stop bothering them." Unfortunately, these thoughts sometimes act as a self-fulfilling prophecy. A person who has these types of thoughts are unlikely to share much about themselves or try to keep the conversation going long enough to deepen a relationship. The result is that other people may perceive them as not wanting to engage in conversation and avoid further interaction.

The way that core beliefs affect our interpretations of the world and our subsequent behaviors is nicely illustrated in the film *Inside Out 2*. At the beginning of the movie, Riley's core belief was that she was inherently a good person. Consistent with this belief, she was kind to others and a fantastic team-player. In the climactic moments of the first hockey game, she chose to pass the puck to her friend instead of hogging the glory and going for an ambitious buzzer beater. Throughout the film, Riley began to go through puberty and a new emotion, Anxiety, began to take greater control of her actions. As a result, she started to prioritize her future high school ambitions at the expense of her current relationships. She also became much more self-critical of her hockey skills and obsessively practiced hockey to become a better player. In a moment of insecurity, she even snuck into her coach's office to see if she made the team. These self-serving behaviors competed with her initial core belief that she was a good person. Ultimately, a second core belief of "I'm not good enough" became more prominent in defining her sense of self. This core belief of ineffectiveness reared its ugly head every time she missed a shot. As a juxtaposition to her first core belief of being a good person, where she passed the puck to her friend to share in the success, this time she stole the puck from her own teammate and accidentally hurt them in the process to show off her skills. This impulsive need to prove herself, even at the expense of her friendships, resulted from the core belief of not being good enough.

Core beliefs bleed into our assumptions about ourselves, others, and the world, which in turn affects how we think about each moment of our lives. It is then arguable that changing core beliefs would likely have the greatest impact on a person's well-being. Of course, the kicker is that core beliefs are also the hardest to change because they are so deeply embedded into our sense of self. Like with Riley, it took many experiences to eventually displace the initial core belief of being a good person to create a new problematic core belief of not being good enough. Therefore, it's often helpful to start working with some of the more surface-level thoughts and assumptions before making our way down to the foundational core.

Cognitive behavioral therapy has no shortage of strategies to target unhelpful thinking patterns. The word cognitions is part of the namesake, after all. As discussed, automatic thoughts are the thoughts that come up naturally in response to a situation. If you recall the example I provided in the first chapter of the book about the friend walking by, there can be many interpretations to this event, such as "they don't like me," "I must have done something wrong," or "they must be busy." When working to change automatic thoughts, it is first helpful to identify the hot thought. The hot thought is the cognition that is tied to the strongest emotions. For example, a thought like "I'm a terrible student" is more likely to be the hot thought than "the test was very hard." In the friend across the street situation, we can assume the thought, "they don't like me" is probably the hot thought because it could be activating a core belief of being unlovable. This type of thought is also known as *mind reading* because we assume that our friend ignored us because they don't like us.

To reframe these hot thoughts, one helpful strategy is to examine the evidence of the thought like one would in a court of law. Imagine that you are in an episode of Judge Judy and all evidence that supports and refutes this thought needs to be admissible in court. If I were to say that I think my friend doesn't like me because I feel it in my gut, I would get a verbal smackdown by Judge Judy. Instead, facts that support my thought would be that the friend indeed did not respond to me at that moment and that he has recently been less responsive to my messages. For evidence against the thought, I might identify times when that friend said something kind to me or recall an instance where a mutual acquaintance told me that this friend has been dealing with personal issues. Once we have the evidence for and against the thought, we can then write out a balanced thought that honors the truth of both sides. For example: "It's possible my friend is mad at me, but he has told me that he enjoys spending time with me." I might also develop a more helpful alternative thought: "Perhaps he is struggling with his own mental health concerns. I can reach out to check in." These thoughts can reduce the emotional intensity that comes with fully investing in the automatic thought. As you can see, in neither case am I being delusional in my reframing; in fact, they are much more grounded in reality than the initial distressing thought.

Underlying automatic thoughts are assumptions and rules about the world. For example, a person with a core belief of being unlovable will go through life with the assumption that other people won't want to spend time with them. These rules are typically fashioned in "if-then" statements. *If* they were to try to make plans with a coworker, *then* they would get rejected. If they were to talk to a stranger at a party, then the other person would ignore them. The way to test assumptions is pretty simple—behavioral experiments! My mind has made an assumption, so why don't I test it? Let's just see what would happen if I were to ask an acquaintance to hang out for drinks. Let's see what happens if I apply for that postgraduate program even if I predict nothing good will come of it. At worst nothing changes. At best we have gathered some conflicting evidence about an assumption that was not serving us. One of my patients held assumptions about needing to put in extra effort at work; otherwise, her bosses would complain about her work quality. Her experiment was simply to reduce her effort to normal levels to test this assumption. Spoiler alert: her good was indeed good enough.

At the bedrock, we need to work on the core beliefs that pervade a person's sense of self. It is possible that by gathering lots of evidence that is contrary to this core belief, such as through restructuring hot thoughts and testing assumptions, that this other work has provided some new nutrients to change the roots of the core belief. One strategy that I have found helpful is to identify past experiences that run contrary to their core belief that patients can use as a base to develop a competing positive core belief. Andre was a patient of mine in a group treatment for depression. His core belief was that he was fundamentally broken. Andre felt helpless in dealing with his depression. He believed that nothing he did could meaningfully change his struggles with mental health. We revisited Andre's past to see if we could identify some examples of when he was able to help himself. Andre came from a Jamaican background and his family held a strong stigma against anything related to mental health. Even though Andre had been dealing with depression for years, his parents discouraged him from seeking mental health services. However, in a moment of courage, Andre decided to find a counsellor despite the influence that his culture and family values had on his life. This was a powerful memory for Andre because it flew in the face of the way he thought about himself. He developed an alternative core belief that he wasn't fundamentally broken; instead, Andre thought of himself as a "work in progress" and there was good evidence that his efforts in therapy were paying off. This competing belief became stronger every time he gathered more evidence of his effectiveness, such as noticing improvements throughout therapy, reconnecting with old hobbies, and continuing to help clients in his work at social services.

Isaac was a patient I saw for social anxiety treatment. He had recently immigrated to Canada from Israel. Isaac had a past course of treatment in social anxiety and he had made good progress to feel more comfortable in social situations. However, the fact that he was now in a foreign environment in Toronto and needing to speak English instead of Hebrew brought back his feelings of discomfort. He felt uncomfortable and incompetent in social situations. As a result, Isaac would try to end conversations as soon as possible because of automatic thoughts such as "they won't understand me because my English is terrible" and "I'm boring." Even in therapy, Isaac would keep casual chit-chat to a minimum and leave as soon as we finished up with the main agenda. He told me that he would often follow social scripts, choosing socially acceptable topics like work, or pull from his "patient script" where he has safe topics to talk about in therapy. The moment the conversation turned more spontaneous, Isaac would try to exit the interaction immediately. Underlying Isaac's automatic thoughts was the assumption that people didn't want to socialize with him and that they wouldn't understand his English well. To evaluate the thought, we gathered evidence on times where people had difficulty understanding him as well as times when he was able to get his point across when he was speaking

English. As part of this process, I was able to even speak to my own experience with him in therapy. I let Isaac know that I thought we understood each other well and I very much enjoyed talking to him because he was equal parts considerate and hilarious. I also told him that I appreciated that he was so mindful of my time by making sure that we always ended the session on time. We came out with a balanced thought that people, myself included, liked talking to him and understood him well. We also simultaneously honored the discomfort that came with speaking a language that is not his native tongue. To test his assumptions that people would not want to engage with him socially, we set up experiments for Isaac to go to game nights and start conversations with strangers (like his Uber driver). Isaac found that he had a lot of fun and meaningful conversations with people from all walks of life. He was a natural conversationalist when he took the leap of faith and decided to be his authentic self. Over time, Isaac made progress toward feeling more competent. Consequently, he was able to bring more of usual lovable and hilarious self into his social interactions.

Thought and behaviors mutually influence each other. Change the behavior and the thoughts change with them. Change the thought and the behaviors are sure to follow. With Isaac, he naturally felt more comfortable maintaining a conversation and bringing in more of himself into social situations as we challenged his thoughts. Additionally, his new behaviors served to obtain additional evidence that his fears were not always true. Isaac rode the positive feedback loop to get out of his mind and into a brighter, more sociable world.

This reframing of thoughts and beliefs can have profound impact even in disorders related to traumatic events. Therapists conceptualize trauma-related concerns as a disorder of non-recovery. Following a traumatic event, the mind and body typically takes time to properly heal. However, in trauma disorders, something gets stuck in the recovery journey and the person is not able to properly process the event. The culprit is something called "stuck points"—negative beliefs that keep a person feeling stuck by profoundly affecting how they view themselves and the world. For example, stuck points can include thoughts that the trauma was their fault or beliefs that other people are not trustworthy. The goal of cognitive processing therapy is to work through these stuck points and manage the difficult emotions associated with these beliefs. I was providing cognitive processing therapy for a patient named Amy who had been sexually assaulted as a teenager. She was working as a babysitter for her neighbor and his daughter. On one occasion, this neighbor stayed at home while Amy was babysitting and started pressuring her to drink alcohol. He had put something in her drink and assaulted her when she was disoriented from the concoction. For many years, Amy blamed herself. She believed herself naive for not reading the danger signals, weak because she didn't fight back, and stupid for staying in the house. These stuck points kept her trapped in the past. Through our work together, we revisited the trauma event. Cognitive processing therapy can include an exposure practice whereby the patient writes out the traumatic event in detail. As we went through Amy's account, we identified from what she wrote that she had actually demonstrated an incredible resilience and awareness during the situation. Unlike what her stuck points suggested, Amy was acutely aware from the beginning that something was wrong and she had called her boyfriend to come get her. Instead of immediately leaving the house, Amy stayed because she was worried for the little girl under the man's care. And she had fought like hell when the man tried to sexually assault her. She remembered that her nails were bloodied from clawing and tearing at her abuser. This exposure practice allowed her to realize that she wasn't any of the things that she initially thought. She was not naive. She was not weak. She was not stupid. Amy came out of this therapy experience with a newfound resilience. From this work, she began to participate in volunteer work to provide support to other women who had gone through similar traumas. She had turned a horrific past event into an incredible strength by becoming a source of support for others as a person who has truly walked a mile in their shoes.

5

It's True but Not Useful

"Your scientists were so preoccupied with whether they could, they didn't stop to think if they should."—Ian Malcolm in *Jurassic Park*

The last chapter focused on testing the truthfulness or "validity" of thoughts. Like lawyers and scientists, we examined the evidence of thoughts and used behavioral experiments to test assumptions. Occasionally, however, thoughts can be true but not helpful. At the sleep health clinic at Stanford, I was working with Aarav—an engineer who struggled with chronic insomnia. Insomnia had been a lifelong concern for Aarav. Unsurprisingly, he spent a lot of time thinking about his insomnia and the factors that could be contributing to his sleep problem. Aarav was very distraught every time he had a bad night and would treat his insomnia like an engineering problem. Was it something he ate? Did he work out too close to his bedtime? Is it possible that there was something fundamentally broken in his brain? What if these sleep problems were causing some sort of major health problem like dementia? The cascade of worries would rush through Aarav's mind all night.

The issue wasn't that these thoughts were necessarily wrong. In fact, all of these thoughts could be true in theory. For example, it is certainly possible that something he ate may have disrupted his sleep. It is also possible that working out too close to bedtime activated his arousal system and made it harder to fall asleep. However, it would be extremely difficult to systematically test all of these worries to be able to conclude exactly what was causing his sleep problems. Therefore, the real problem was not one of validity. Rather, the problem was one of utility. The fact of the matter was that these thoughts just weren't helpful toward Aarav's goal of sleeping well. In my mind, these worry thoughts only served to increase Aarav's anxiety and made his mind race throughout the night. It is quite challenging to whisk an active mind away into dreamland. When Aarav finally finished going through his laundry list of possible reasons for his poor sleep, he asked me what I thought might be the cause of his insomnia. I gestured to the top of his head and said that if I were a betting man, I'd think it was probably the worrying itself!

The case example illustrates that idea that thoughts can be true but not helpful. The focus on utility rather than validity is important to engender flexibility in the way that we operate in life. Sometimes we get so stuck in being right that we lose sight of our goals. There is a concept in dialectical behavior therapy known as "effectiveness." Effectiveness is not worried about what is right; instead, effectiveness is only concerned about whether thoughts or behaviors are helpful in moving toward one's goals. In Aarav's case, his goal was to get a good night's sleep. However, his constant worrying made him more restless at night and paradoxically made it harder to sleep. Consequently, this worrying was not particularly effective in support of his goal.

In effectiveness, the optimal behavior will vary based on the goal. If Aarav's goal was to simply outline all possible reasons why people can have poor sleep, then perhaps this type of worrying would be considered effective. This idea can be applied into other contexts as well. For example, thoughts like "the world is unfair" or "people should treat other people nicer" are true. However, if these thoughts make us put in less effort to achieve our goals or stop us from developing meaningful relationships, then they become unhelpful. I agree that there are systemic reasons why some people have it much harder than others. This absolutely needs to be acknowledged. But when these judgments about how things "should be" take attention away from how things are in reality, we cannot act effectively. In fact, we are turning away from reality. Instead, I encourage you to let your goals dictate your behaviors and thoughts. As I noted, when considering the most effective course of action, there is no specific strategy that is always effective; this varies based on your goals. If your goal is to have everyone remember your birthday, then sending fifty messages a day to everybody on your contact list may technically be effective. In most cases, you probably would want to maintain a good relationship with your friends and not annoy the living heck out of them. In this case, you might simply mention your upcoming birthday in passing during hangouts. I invite you to think about your own goals and whether your behaviors are the most effective path toward them.

With Aarav, he began to understand that his worrying was not helpful toward his goal of sleeping better. In a turn of irony, Aarav realized that his desire to solve his insomnia problem was the exact thing stopping him from having a better night. It was indeed possible that his worries were true. However, this worrying certainly didn't solve any problems. Instead, they simply exacerbated his fears and made it harder for him to sleep. Instead of putting effort on worrying, Aarav began to follow the recommendations we discussed and let sleep take him away.

In considering the value of a thought, I invite you to ask yourself two questions. First, is the thought true? Second, even if the thought is true, is it helpful? At the end of the day, thoughts are simply thoughts. They are not facts, and we do not have to treat them as though they were gospel. This is especially true when the thoughts are not grounded in reality or when they are not helpful in supporting our well-being. Sometimes we feel fused with our thoughts and it is hard to create psychological distance from them. In those moments, the thoughts feel overwhelmingly real and we feel compelled to act in accordance with the thoughts. One strategy to create some distance between you and the thought is through mindful imagery. If you are a visual person, see if you can treat those thoughts as though you were observing them as leaves on the river or clouds in the sky. Just letting them float away. If you are a person who has a hard time with imagery, you can even create distance by stating "I had a thought right now." You could even repeat the thoughts in different voices, like in the voice of Tweety Bird or SpongeBob. These practices externalizes the thought and creates distance from the thought in order to be able to evaluate them more objectively. And if you find that the thought isn't particularly enjoyable or useful, simply let it float away.

6

The Art of Problem-Solving

"Just do it."—Nike

A common though unsubstantiated criticism of therapy is that it is just all talk and gets you nowhere outside of the therapy room. Some joke that a therapist is just going to ask you to take a walk if you are depressed. I disagree on both counts. I believe therapists work to support change at a deeper level and help address the barriers that keep a person feeling stuck. For some disorders like depression, even getting out of bed can be a Herculean task, and nothing—not even the longest, most fulfilling walk in the world—feels like it will help. In these moments of despair, it can be invalidating for somebody to tell them to just take a walk, even if the walk might be helpful.

In his book, *The Gift of Therapy*, Irvin Yalom recommended therapists to "strike when the iron is cold." This is because it is hard for patients to internalize lessons when they are in the eye of the emotional storm. Therefore, the therapist's role is to help the patient process emotions with the much-needed validation and compassion to cool the iron. After that, sometimes the next step is as simple as starting to take that walk or return a friend's call. Instead of scoffing at that idea, isn't it great that something so trivial can have such outsized returns on your life? Consequently, therapy is kind of about and not about taking the walk. The therapist helps patients with the implementation by addressing the barriers that get in the way of actions toward their goals. We can talk forever about the gaping hole in front of us on our journey up the mountain. At the end of the day, however, we will still need to build the bridge to get to the top.

Just like in dialectical behavior therapy, there is a balance that needs to be struck between acceptance and change. In situations that are unavoidable and cannot be controlled, it makes good sense to validate the emotions resulting from hardships and take an acceptance stance. However, in other cases, the problem just needs to be solved. For example, if you remember my patient Avery, they had returned to school after an extended break for mental health reasons. However, they were procrastinating on assignments despite the looming deadline. In this case, the assignments needed to be finished in order to pass their courses and obtain a college degree. As the therapist, my role would be to work with Avery in identifying and resolving the obstacles getting in the way of completing their work.

There are two levels to problem-solving. The first is to plan out the problem and solution and the second is to address the barriers in order to successfully implement the solution into your life. Problem-solving can be pretty simple. In many cases, there is no need to go through a formal process to figure out a solution. For example, the problem might simply be resolved with a quick phone call or setting up an appointment. However, there are situations where it would be helpful to apply a step-by-step approach to problem-solving.

The first step is to identify the problem. What problem are you trying to solve? Afterward, you write down the desired outcome. What is the desired end result? To determine possible actions, you then take some time to brainstorm different solutions. Be non-judgmental here and just let any and all ideas fall onto the page. You then systematically evaluate each solution by writing down the pros and cons for each solution. Pick the best one from the batch, do the thing, and then reflect on how it went. Easy-peasy.

Let's work through an example of this problem-solving process. You have a nice weekend date planned with your partner to rekindle the romantic spark, which has been slightly dimmed after having spent the last several years working together to take care of your now five-year-old son. The problem is that you want this trip to be just about you two, however, you don't have childcare for the weekend. Since three's a crowd, the desired outcome is you find somebody to take care of tiny Timmy so you can enjoy your weekend vacation as a couple. You brainstorm some ideas and come up with a few potential solutions: (1) You could hire a babysitter, (2) you could ask your parents or in-laws, (3) you could bring him with you, or (4) you could leave him at home by himself (probably not the best idea unless you're looking for a rehash of *Home Alone*—but we're also being non-judgmental in this step!). After considering the pros and cons of each option, let's say you decide to ask your parents to take care of your son for the weekend. Ideally, they say yes and everything is good in the hood. If not, then you might turn toward the drawing board and pick your second-best choice.

I went through a simple example above just to showcase the steps of problem-solving in greater detail. However, there are some problems that are more challenging to implement into our lives for one reason or another. For example, let's say your goal is to be more social or active, but you're struggling with getting started. Now what?

The use of SMART goals can be a helpful skill in these scenarios. SMART stands for *s*pecific, *m*easurable, *a*chievable, *r*elevant, and *t*ime-bound. Goals such as "being more active" or "being happy" are excellent, but they are not particularly specific. You can put a dozen people in a room and each of them will give you a different definition of what it means to be happy or active. A more specific goal of being active would be something like running for an hour a day in the morning. However, this goal might not be achievable if you have been struggling with depression and have been in potato mode for the better part of a decade. A SMART goal could be starting with a 15-minute walk three times over the week, which is more likely to set you up for success. In this case, the goal is specific, achievable, relevant to the goal of being more active, you'll know when it's done (time-bound), and you can even rate how you feel afterward (measurable).

You will need to be your own therapist to identify possible barriers that get in the way of achieving your goals and plan for contingencies to stack the cards in your favor. For example, one obstacle that could foil your plans to take a jog after work is coming home to rest for a moment only for the gravitational pull from the La-Z-Boy recliner to suck you in and keep you stuck for the rest of the evening. Instead of falling for the La-Z-Boy trap, you might decide to put on your runners and immediately leave for your run. This removes inertia as a factor in stopping you from your goals. You could also reinforce the jog by planning to enjoy a new episode of your favorite show when you come home. Let's say that your goal is to walk in the morning, but the problem is that you tend to unconsciously hit the snooze button far too often. This can be problem-solved by placing the alarm a little further away from the bed so you have to get up to shut the alarm. When I have difficulty getting motivated for a gym session, my go-to strategy is to take a pre-workout supplement in the form of an artificially flavored drink. Drinking this weird concoction is something that is reinforcing because it is tasty and I like the jittery feeling. Once I have taken the pre-workout drink, my thoughts shift from "I don't want to go because I'm too tired" to "well, I might as well go because I would feel awkward sitting in my chair with the tingling sensations all over my body." You may have to reframe unhelpful thoughts, such as "there's no point" or "I won't feel better anyways." In response, you might put on your curious scientist hat and conduct a small behavioral experiment just to see if you actually feel worse after the run. If you know the exact reason why something is preventing you from reaching your goal, then you can take a precise approach to overcoming the obstacle.

With my patient Avery, they had returned to school with the goal of graduating to feel more stable in their life. The problem was that they were constantly avoiding their assignments. The desired outcome was obvious: Get the work done. The problem was that whenever Avery got in front of their computer, they would feel very distressed. Thoughts like "I'm so stupid" and "I won't understand" pervaded their mind each time Avery could not immediately figure out the answer. The feeling of "not-knowing" was generating a lot of shame. As a result, Avery would deal with these aversive emotions through distraction strategies—namely an unhealthy dose of TikTok and Instagram. Together, we worked on sitting with those feelings of shame in order for Avery to process these emotions and focus on their work. With practice Avery realized that once the initial distress reduced, they actually understood the material quite well and they were able to start working on the assignments. In Avery's case, the obstacle was aversive emotions related to shame, so the way to get over this obstacle was through exposure practice and learning to tolerate these feelings.

When it comes to problem-solving, some problems and solutions are obvious. If your car is running low on gas, there is no need to bring in Sherlock Holmes to solve the issue. However, other situations are trickier, like whether you should stand up for yourself when a friend is constantly asking you for favors. Perhaps this friend has helped you out in the past and you feel guilty rejecting their request. In this case, we aren't sure if there is truly a problem and whether a solution is required. One place where we draw wisdom to answer this question is by listening to our emotions. Emotions tell us something about ourselves and our needs. For example, anger tells us that a boundary has been crossed. Sadness says we have lost something. Anxiety lets us know that there is a threat present. Guilt informs us that we have done something wrong. When the emotions fit the facts of the situation, then we need to work to change the situation and problem-solve. For example, if we are feeling guilty because we made an insensitive comment to our friend in the heat of the moment, then the solution would be to apologize to that person. Here's another example. Let's say you have a deadline coming up for a work project that you have been working on for the past year with your team. However, you have yet to even start developing the pitch deck for your presentation with the board of directors next Monday. In this case, it would make very good sense that you feel anxious and there is definitely a problem that needs to be solved. Going back to the first scenario, let's say the reason the friend is upset is because you set a boundary and finally said no to their request for money. The emotion of guilt does not necessarily fit the facts. Instead of problem-solving, we can prioritize working on the emotion of guilt. This is because there is no problem to solve; you simply prioritized yourself and set a boundary. The "checking of the facts" helped to recognize that the guilt was not substantiated. You shouldn't feel bad about prioritizing your own needs, especially when the other person has not reciprocated your generosity and kindness. Therefore, it is your guilt that is not justified in this scenario. Of course, you can still feel guilty (it's normal to have an emotional response), but you should not listen to what the guilt is telling you to do, which is to apologize and give them more money.

I invite you to consider for a moment if there are problems in your life that could benefit from a little resolution. It may be an obvious problem, such as needing to set an appointment or send off an email. In cases where you know obstacles will present themselves, I encourage you to be your own therapist and set yourself up for success through SMART goals to break the task down into more manageable and actionable steps. If you are unsure whether there is actually a problem that needs to be solved, you can check in with your emotions and determine whether the facts support how you are feeling. Start with something small and do it to get the ball rolling. Starting is often the hardest part, so make the start the smallest step. Momentum begets momentum. If you need to get an assignment done, then maybe just start with opening the document. If you want to take that walk then start by just putting on your shoes. With all that said, go on that damn walk!

7

Pavlov's Dog and Skinner's Rats

"An individual's behavior is shaped by the consequences of that behavior."—B.F. Skinner

Behaviorists, as their name suggests, focus on behaviors. They considered the mind and its contents (thoughts, beliefs, repressed memories) as a "black box"—internal processes that cannot be measured. Given that these phenomena could not be observed, they could not be placed under scientific investigation. The behaviorists therefore decided to ignore them. Behaviors, on the other hand, are absolutely measurable. We can't be sure what a rat is thinking but we can certainly see how many times the rat presses a button.

B.F. Skinner was an American psychologist that was famous for his study of animal behavior and the use of the infamous Skinner box. The box is a small, enclosed space where an animal is placed within to interact with objects in the environment, such as a lever. Pushing the lever offered a reward such as food or provided a punishment like an electric shock. This work, known as operant conditioning, contributed to our understanding of learning principles and how behaviors change based on its consequences. Specifically, two such consequences include reinforcements, which served to increase the frequency of a behavior, and punishments, which served to decrease behaviors. Reinforcements could be positive, adding something that is desirable, or negative, taking away something that is causing aversive feelings. An example of negative reinforcement would be smoking a cigarette to get rid of cravings. A person is therefore reinforced to continue smoking in order to keep the bad feelings away.

This understanding of the relationship between behaviors and consequences also informed models of mental disorders like depression. Martin Seligman conducted studies on dogs and assessed what would happen if they were exposed to uncontrollable electric shocks. No matter what the dogs did they would continue to be punished with the aversive shocks. After instilling a sense of helplessness in the dogs, Seligman then placed the dogs in a box where it was possible to escape from the electric shocks. However, what he found was that the dogs made no efforts to escape and continued to passively endure their mild form of torture.

Seligman coined this phenomenon learned helplessness. This is a condition that arises from a history of perceived failure even in the presence of significant effort. As a result, a person (or dog) develops a lack of self-efficacy in influencing the trajectory of their life and decides to stop trying altogether. Learned helplessness may contribute to depression because people feel a lack of control in their life. After all, there is nothing they can do to get out of their situation and the world seems unlikely to help.

The therapeutic implications behind operant learning is that we can change the likelihood of engaging in effective behaviors through managing the consequences. For example, if I reward myself with a skittle every time I write a sentence, then I am likely to continue putting down more words on the page. This is called token economy where we receive a reward (skittle) for a desired behavior (writing). However, if I were to constantly think about how much more I have to write, which could be rather punishing, then I may feel too distressed to keep writing. It is important to figure out what are personal reinforcers and punishers in your life. For example, let's say your goal is to get up at 7:00 a.m. consistently. An example of positive reinforcement may be the hot coffee that is waiting for you made by your lovely spouse. An example of a negative reinforcement could be your alarm, placed far away and made as obnoxious as possible, so that forces you to get out of bed to close the alarm providing you relief from its incessant blaring. A form of punishment could be that your spouse won't give you a morning kiss if you don't get up at 7:00 a.m. Whatever works.

The use of reinforcements can also be very helpful in interpersonal relationships. In fact, reinforcements are a key component of interpersonal effectiveness in dialectical behavior therapy. The acronym for effective communication is called DEAR: describe, express, assert, and reinforce. The DEAR skill is meant to guide people to clearly describe a situation factually, express their feelings about the issue, assert their needs, and reinforce the other person to accept their demands. For example, let's say you recently started a new romantic relationship. Things are generally going well and your new flame has expressed that they are interested in being in a serious relationship with you. However, they rarely take the initiative in the relationship. You are understandably feeling a little hurt given the perceived lack of effort. A DEAR statement could be something along the lines of: "I've noticed that I am usually the person planning date nights and finding ways to spend more time together (Describe). This makes me feel like I am less of a priority in your life (Express). I would like for you to text me and plan date nights more often (Assert). I am also looking for something serious and I would feel more comfortable deepening our relationship if I saw more initiative (Reinforce)."

When engaging in assertive communication, it is important for the other person to be reinforced to engage in the behavior. In this example, the other person wishes for a more serious relationship. Consequently, the behavior of taking more initiative to plan dates is reinforced by highlighting how a change in behavior could support the other person's desires. When engaging in effective communication, it is important to be mindful of your own goals. You may have a script but the other person does not and their response may take you into foreign territory. Consequently, there may be a need to be like a "broken record" and continue expressing your needs (negotiating as needed).

Another learning principle commonly used in therapy besides

operant conditioning is classical conditioning. This concept might "ring a bell" (ha-ha terrible pun) because I discussed classical conditioning in Kate's story about insomnia. Just like spending time in bed feeling frustrated can create conditioned arousal, we can associate situations with specific feelings and behaviors. For example, if we spent a lot of our early years drinking alcohol in dorm rooms, the brain creates an association between these two things. Visiting your old dorm room may elicit an urge to use alcohol because of classical conditioning. One of my patients had a goal to reduce his smoking. Through our analyses, we identified a number of places associated with smoking when he was taking his dog for a morning walk, like the mart where he purchases cigarettes and the park where he typically stops to take a smoke. As a form of stimulus control, we got him to plan out a different route where the landmarks were not associated with smoking.

I encourage you to take these learning principles and apply them to your life. Discipline is great but we do not have to make hard work unnecessarily hard. Instead of using all of our mental resources fighting against the current, we can leverage classical and operant conditioning to ride the wave instead. This might mean conditioning a specific room that is enjoyable for work. You might create a playlist specific for work, place some lovely flowers in the room, and sit near a window where you can get some sunlight. For healthy sleep habits, it may mean protecting the bedroom as a place for relaxation and sleep rather than spending time worrying or working in bed. In terms of operant conditioning, you can leverage reinforcements and punishments to support movement toward goals. Make the good stuff as easy as possible to do, and the not-so-good stuff as hard to do as possible. As James Clear once said in his book *Atomic Habits*: "You do not rise to the level of your goals. You fall to the level of your systems."

8

Remembering to Smell the Roses

"I'm going on an adventure!"—Bilbo Baggins in *The Hobbit*

I'll start this chapter with a story based on a really cool video made by Russ Harris—one of the foremost practitioners of acceptance and commitment therapy. In the story, there are two kids in a car heading to Disneyland. We will call them Carter and Lee. Carter is ecstatic about the idea of going to Disneyland. It's only been about 20 minutes since they left the house, but Carter is already tired of the boring ride known as his dad's 2016 Nissa Versa and is ready to hop on Space Mountain and Rise of the Resistance. He wants to trade in the playlist on his dad's classic rock cassette for the symphony of music at the happiest place on Earth. He relishes the moment when he is finally able to devour a cheesy garlic pretzel bread from Maurice's Treats. Unfortunately for Carter, he suffered from a mind-body problem: His mind could travel into the future but his body was stuck in the present. And there was still about a half-day drive until they reached Disneyland. Carter is feeling rather impatient—each red light feels like purgatory and every second ticks away with excruciating agony. If anything were to get in the way of him and Disneyland, there would absolutely be hell to pay in Carter's mind.

Lee, on the other hand, is also looking forward to Disneyland. He is excited to try out all the wonderful attractions, sample the delicious foods, and relax at the resort. But Lee also finds moments of joy in the trip. For example, he likes to observe the surrounding landscape and the interchange of urban and nature scenery throughout the drive. He enjoys jamming to his dad's classic rock playlist, especially "Have You Ever Seen the Rain" by Creedence Clearwater Revival. Lee simply enjoys spending time with his dad and brother.

The difference between Lee and Carter is that whereas Carter is focused only on the destination, Lee finds pleasure in the journey. Even if Disneyland happened to be closed for the day, Lee—albeit disappointed—would still find meaning in his time spent with his brother and dad. Carter would likely find the cancellation a tragedy and develop a core memory of a time when the world failed him.

In therapy, I sometimes talk about the difference between outcome and process. Humans are often very outcome-focused by nature. We decide whether something was worthwhile through analyzing the end product. However, focusing solely on the outcome is tricky because the outcomes are not always within our control. Not even Steph Curry can hit a three-pointer every time. However, if we focus only on making the shot, then we can be emotionally impacted by the fickleness of the outcome. For example, a person with depression might have thoughts of worthlessness every time they receive poor marks on an exam. An individual with social anxiety might think that their attempt to start a conversation was a failure whenever somebody doesn't bust a gut laughing at their jokes. In contrast, process-oriented people place their worth on their actions rather than the goal itself. They find meaning in studying hard for the exam or plucking up the courage to start a conversation in spite of their anxiety. Therefore, they place value in something that is fully controllable. We can't always make the basket but we can always take the shot. These are the Lees of the world who enjoy the journey rather than the Carters that fixate on their own version of Disneyland.

Over the years, I have worked on becoming more of a process-oriented person. When I was young, I focused mostly on the end result. I needed good grades and an acceptance to my dream program to feel good about myself. I had to win the game of Mario Kart to have fun. I wanted the girl across the lab from me to say yes when I asked her out. I placed my self-worth on these outcomes. And if things didn't work out, I was a failure. This was a problem because things didn't work out on the regular. Nowadays, I put weight into what I can control. When I applied for my postdoctoral fellowship, I wasn't particularly worried about whether the admission committee decided to let me in or not. I was already proud of myself for taking the courageous step to apply for the program. When I wrote this book, I wasn't particularly concerned whether an agent would want to represent me or if the book would eventually be published. I felt accomplished knowing that I was the kind of person who could put the time and effort into writing every day in spite of the uncertainty. Even for my dissertation, I went into the defense focused on the process rather than outcome. I knew that people could have very different reactions to reaching the top of the educational mountain. For many folks, they are excited for the prospect of graduating. They relish the moment when they can finally feel the immense relief of knowing they are finished. They have waited for this moment forever and have spent years drenching each page of their lengthy dissertation with blood, sweat, and tears. And finally, when the dissertation committee welcomes them back into the room after a grueling three-hour defense, calling them by the prefix that they have been waiting to hear for the better part of a decade, the sweet melodious sound of "Doctor"—it falls flat. "Was that it? The culmination of years of toiling. Now what?" For many people, there can be a sort of existential discomfort that comes from finally reaching the top of the mountain and wondering where to go from there.

For me, I knew going into the dissertation defense that my feelings would probably be the same. It'd be like feeling parched on a summer's day, taking a sip of Cherry Coke and realizing the drink is lukewarm. However, I was appreciative of the journey. I was able to do a bunch of cool stuff and travel to various places to present my research (and goof off). In graduate school, I had a lot of flexibility in my work schedule. I could try out new restaurants at 2:00 p.m. on a random Tuesday or hit the gym after a lab meeting. I was able to work with so many intelligent and compassionate people. I loved the journey so I didn't particularly mind the destination. And I was right. I didn't feel much at the end of the doctoral defense. I was still on my clinical internship until the end of the month and I had to plan my move to California for the postdoctoral fellowship. But even without these things on my mind, I suspect that my conclusion would not be like Thanos at the end of *Infinity War*, watching the sun rise on a grateful universe following a job well done. However, it was still nice to watch the metaphorical ending credits roll on the movie known as graduate school. I also got a hazelnut cream cheese bagel as a treat afterward. It was tasty.

When we focus just on the outcome, the pleasure and fulfilment is fleeting and often underwhelming. There is always a new mountain to climb. We humans are just built that way. Don't get me wrong, the outcome is important in many ways. At the end of the day, we need to be successful in getting a job to put food on the table and have our crush agree to a date to move toward our own (hopefully) happily-ever-after. Still, I try to place my value within the effort of my actions rather than the outcome itself. For the book, I succeed when I put words on the page. For career opportunities, I succeed when I put in the effort to prepare well and apply for the position. For my moderate social anxiety, I succeed when I cobble together the courage to ask the waitress for another napkin. For me, there is meaning in the doing. The outcome matters less because going on the journey was the important part. A good outcome then just simply becomes the cherry on top.

I've found this process-oriented approach a lot more conducive to happiness and improved self-worth. It is significantly more within my control when I measure success with the doing rather than the achieving. One example is to place importance in applying to a new job rather than getting hired. The decision to apply is fully controllable. However, the employer deciding to hire you is not. Many factors can play a role for whether or not somebody gets hired: The fit between the applicant's skills and employer's needs, whether the company already had someone else in mind and this application process was just empty bureaucracy, or perhaps the interviewer decided they needed someone of a specific demographic profile. There are a million possible reasons. As commander Jean-Luc Picard once said: "It is possible to commit no mistakes and still lose. That is not a weakness; that is life." In this case, however, we can just focus on doing the right things as the condition for victory.

Again, when I write this book, I enjoy the process of writing itself. I value being able to synthesize ideas together into a coherent narrative and communicate them to other people. I enjoy being able to create something that hopefully provides some use for someone out there in the world. However, my happiness is not tied to the outcome. It would be nice for an agent to represent me and a publishing house to take a chance on the book. It would also be nice to have people decide to pick it out of the shelf. And it would most certainly be wonderful to have readers feel like they took something away from this book that benefited their lives. I don't pretend to not care at all about the outcome. But the main point was the process. I wanted to be the type of person that is able to commit to something for a prolonged period of time. To bring my clinical experiences and education together and create something that was wholly mine. And to write for the sake of writing.

As a result, I certainly have my own extensive catalogue of writing projects that have never seen the light of day. For example, I have manuscripts that I had written with the intention of publication in academic journals disappear into the file drawer because the reviewers did not think that findings were particularly interesting to publish. If my goal was simply to be published, then the time and effort I spent writing these papers would feel utterly meaningless. I would reasonably feel quite disappointed. However, I don't regret that time at all. It was still fun to think and write. Moreover, I don't consider effort to be ever truly meaningless. It is absolutely possible that something I wrote that initially had zero traction eventually become the backbone of a future project. I'm not a fortune-teller, so it would be pretty arrogant of me to wave away the potential utility of the work that I did just because I can't see its impact at the moment. Even if not readily visible, this work may have improved my writing, the way I think, and the way I deal with setbacks.

Besides writing projects, I'm sure there are many examples of work that I have done that others may consider completely meaningless. During the data analysis phase of my dissertation, I spent hours on monkey work entering data point after data point. The research was on teen sleep health and students from a partnering high school had tracked their sleep to study the potential benefits of a teen sleep app on their sleep habits. There were hundreds of students who participated in the study. Each student completed about a month's worth of sleep diaries and each day had a dozen rows of data points. Some quick calculations indicate around 100,000 data points that I entered by hand over the period of a couple months. Now, a smarter person than I could have probably figured out some sort of coding wizardry and compiled the data in an afternoon. Given my lack of ability, and general laziness to think of a smarter, more efficient solution, I decided to just brute force the whole operation. It would be very reasonable to say that I wasted all that time if another person was able to develop a code to do in a fraction of the time. However, I found something about the process to be innately enjoyable and worthwhile. For one, it was a surprisingly pleasant routine to wake up before work at the hospital, head over to a nearby coffee shop, and start inputting numbers on my computer next to a cup of medium roast coffee and a blueberry scone. The ambience was cozy and enjoyable, and the work—while tedious—made me feel oddly productive. This work also allowed me to practice being comfortable sitting with the mundane. And if I could inject life into something so mindless, how wonderful could life be when I was actually doing something more interesting? Consequently, I gave the work itself meaning rather than focusing on the future of a finished dissertation. I threw myself into the task. Surprisingly, the process turned out pretty fun.

One of my patients, Andy, was a very outcome-focused guy. He was a young professional in his early thirties working in investment banking. His emphasis on the results paid dividends and took him far in his career. However, the daily hassles of work itself were stressful and painful. Andy didn't enjoy a lot of things about his current job. Moreover, he also felt discomfort in the process of acclimating to his new role; he felt huge pressure to get up to speed in his role as soon as possible. Alongside reducing his workload to prioritize his other values, Andy was also open to finding ways to make the job itself more meaningful. Together, we asked the question of whether there were parts of his job that could be connected to his larger set of values so he could enjoy the climb up the mountain. Through our discussion, Andy was able to identify that the discomfort itself was meaningful because it meant he was being challenged to grow into his new position. If he felt fully comfortable, then he was no longer meeting his value of growth. To reduce some of his work-related stress, we also identified that Andy's beliefs about not meeting expectations were not rooted in reality to not meeting expectations were not rooted in reality. In fact, there was good evidence that his bosses and colleagues thought he was performing well.

Some folks might think it is silly to just focus on the journey because the world doesn't revolve around the journey; it is about the destination. We can talk all we want about finding meaning in the hard work, but if we don't get the grades, the job, the date, then it is ultimately meaningless. Personally, I think there is beauty in the doing regardless of the outcome. However, even if we are interested in the outcome, I still think there is a strong rationale to focus on the process. Paradoxically, I am of the opinion that focusing on the process increases our chance of a positive outcome. When we prioritize the process, we feel less discouraged by negative outcomes and become better able to stay resilient in the face of perceived failure. We remain steadfast in continuing to take shots until we finally score. I have personally found the most success in my life when I simply focused on doing the right things every day. Instead of worrying about whether or not I was good enough to win an award, I simply applied. Rather than panicking about whether I would be accepted for the fellowship, I just made the submission. I won the award and I ended up going on fellowship. It's like the difference between expending all your effort on forcing someone to like you versus focusing on being the best version of yourself. In the former case, trying to get someone to like you is unlikely to work and might even repel them. However, if you focus on becoming the best version of yourself, it's possible that the other person might take notice of your great qualities. Of course, you'll probably still have to ask the person out unless you are Captain America levels of cool. But even if they say no, you continued doing the important things and moved closer to your ideal self in the process. Another example I can think of where the process leads to better outcome is in bodybuilding. I believe it is the people who truly enjoy the process of bodybuilding who are likely to stay committed for a long enough time to really reap the benefits. Most folks can agree that consistency is one of the most important factors to really develop size and strength. And it is those who truly love the process who can stay committed for the longest time. Of course, there are other factors like genetics that determine who reaches the top of the professional world, but I believe incredible results can come simply from consistency and really enjoying the journey. In general, my belief is that given sufficient time and effort, the chance of a positive outcome is all but guaranteed. However, even in cases where we don't reach our exact destination, perhaps it doesn't matter because we truly enjoyed the journey.

Acceptance and commitment therapy (ACT) is a very process-oriented treatment. A big part of ACT is its emphasis on the present moment and our values. Although we may dream about the future or ruminate on the past, we only truly exist in the here-and-now. If we only focus on our own version of Disneyland while sitting in the car, then we are not living in the present moment. In the story, Lee chooses to enjoy the present moment and be with his family despite being excited for Disneyland. Just the same, we can align our actions in the here-and-now with our values and let future outcomes be secondary gains to the right present-moment behaviors. I believe personal meaning and fulfillment is tucked inside the process. When we think about the hero's journey, we cheer for Hercules not because he is naturally strong, but because we see him toil through the 12 Labors. We are not invested in Spiderman until we watch Peter Parker's story that culminates in him taking a leap of faith and accepting his destiny. There is meaning in the adventure, so take some time to enjoy watching your own story unfold. Regardless of the outcome, you'll still come back to a hero's welcome.

9

Taking a Mindful Moment

> *"It is not things that upset us, it is our judgments of them."*
> —Epictetus

Allow me to invite you to a brief practice. I'd like you to find an object next to you—a pen, a coffee mug, a stuffed toy, whatever is in arm's reach—and I want you to imagine you are observing this object for the first time. You might pretend that you are an alien who just came to this blue-green planet from outer space. This item is completely foreign to your reality. I want you to observe the shape, the colors, the different parts of this object. Use your hand (or alien appendage) and take hold of the object. Feel the texture and see if the physical sensation differs based on the part of the object you are touching. As you interact with this object, pay attention to the different sounds coming from it. Take notice of any smells, maybe there is a distinct odor or perhaps it is odorless. If you're in a particularly adventurous mood, you may even give it a lick and see how it tastes.

There's an inherent sense of wonder that comes about taking a beginner's mind to something that you have seen a million times before and treating the experience as if it were the first. We let go of preconceived notions about the object. We are not imposing our own judgments and biases; we are simply observing reality as it is. This experiential practice is a common one in mindfulness. And in this chapter, I discuss the power and beauty that comes with cultivating a mindful approach to life.

Jon Kabat-Zinn, the creator of the mindfulness-based stress reduction program, defines mindfulness as the "awareness that arises from paying attention to the present moment in a particular way, on purpose, and without judgment." Let's distill this idea into its constituent parts. First, mindfulness is present-focused. We are not ruminating about the past nor worrying about the future. We are right here in the here-and-now. Second, this awareness of the present moment is intentional. We are making a commitment to be present regardless of the nature of the experience, pleasurable or painful. Finally, mindfulness is non-judgmental. Just like an alien seeing something for the first time, we do not place our subjective values into an objective experience. We are not deciding whether something is good or bad; we simply experience it as is.

Most things are inherently neutral. For example, if the weather is sunny, then that means the sun is fully visible and not obstructed by clouds. If it is raining, then that just means there is water in the form of little droplets falling upon our heads. However, we often place judgments into the weather. We judge the sunny California day to be good and the rainy Vancouver mornings to be bad. We think that the mark we received on our physics exam is horrible. We may even judge ourselves as worthless for our poor performance. We also place our demands on reality, like "the world ought to be a certain way" or "other people should be kinder." Although these thoughts may be valid, they create a disparity between reality and expectation and only serve to make us feel worse.

Human life is full of judgments about our experience. As Stoic philosopher Epictetus once said, it is these judgments, rather than the events themselves, that upset us. Receiving sixty percent on an exam is simply a mathematical proportion of correct to incorrect answers. But we might place a judgment of "bad" onto this experience and feel depressed. These judgments turn pain into suffering. I think of pain as an experience that is inherent to life whereas suffering occurs when we resist the experience of pain. For example, chronic pain, as the term suggests, is inherently painful. But if we react to this experience with thoughts such as "Why is my life like this?" and "I feel so hopeless" then these thoughts turn pain into suffering. We suffer twice: Once from the pain and a second time from our reaction to the pain. The idea behind mindfulness is to recognize that reality is not swayed by "shoulds." It simply is. And things are neither good nor bad. They simply are. This is not to say that we cannot have preferences or work to change our lives for the better. Instead, mindfulness simply means that we are attempting to be non-judgmental and to be actively present in reality.

The benefits of mindfulness are expansive. Research suggests that mindfulness enhances self-awareness and fosters a sense of connection with the world; mindfulness improves mood, reduces anxiety, and is conducive to sleep; and mindfulness cultivates a sense of joy and positive well-being. You could randomly choose any aspect of health and I would not be surprised if there was evidence of mindfulness playing a beneficial role. The most incredible thing is that mindfulness can be easily integrated into your life. Case in point, I invite you to simply take a moment and look out your window and find a nearby tree. Spend a few moments to intentionally observe the tree—the trunk, the branches, the leaves—and stay present in beholding its majesty. That's mindfulness.

To further define mindfulness, dialectical behavioral therapy breaks mindfulness in terms of the "what" and the "how." That is, what are we doing when we practice mindfulness and how do we practice these skills? In terms of what to do, the three activities are observe, describe, and participate. Observe includes taking notice of what's going on around you in the present moment. It can be external, such as sensations that your five senses are picking up (e.g., sounds, smells, sights, touch, or taste) or it can be internal (e.g., your thoughts, emotions, or physical sensations). Describe involves putting words to what you have observations. For example, describing the sights (e.g., "I am seeing a large tree with bright yellow leaves and a jagged trunk") or physical sensations (e.g., "I am noticing that there is a lot of tension in my neck," "my breathing feels shallow and quick"). In this case, you might "observe" the sensation of anxiety in your body and then describe it: "I'm noticing that my heart is racing and my stomach's tight." Observe and describe appear similar, but they are different processes. It's like the difference between hearing a bird chirp and then labelling it as a chirp. The third activity, participate means completely throwing yourself into a single activity. This might be dancing to music, eating a meal, playing the piano, among an infinite number of possibilities. In this case, we are not on autopilot like we tend to be when walking or driving. We are not worrying about the future or reminiscing about the past. We are wholly focused on the present activity.

The "How" skills in mindfulness offer instructions on the ways that you can engage in the "What" activities. They include non-judgmentally, one-mindfully, and effectively. When you are observing or describing your experiences, I invite you to take a non-judgmental approach. For example, "I am noticing that the chair I am sitting on is rough" is a non-judgmental description of your experience. In contrast, "This chair is so hard. It's irritating and I hate it" would be a judgmental description of your experience and would likely increase distress. Engaging in an activity one-mindfully means that you are fully focused on the specific task in front of you. If you are reading, then you are focused on the task of reading. Many people like to multitask and engage in several activities simultaneously. It's also not uncommon for some folks to plan their day while engaging in their chores. Although some people find this multitasking to be efficient, it is not a mindful practice. Even if you don't do every task one-mindfully, I encourage you to occasionally throw yourself into an activity, like listening to music, eating a meal, or reading this book. Finally, effectively means that you are always mindful of your goals. If your goal is to practice mindfulness, then make an active intention to stay in the present moment. If something takes you away from the present, that's okay, simply bring your attention back when you notice that it has gone elsewhere. However, if your goal is to distract yourself from an unpleasant activity like cleaning, then it would make sense to listen to music or think about the great fun that you will have with your friend after you finish your chores. This can also apply to other areas of your life. For example, if your goal is to maintain a positive relationship with your partner, then you might decide not to respond with sarcasm during an argument and instead provide validation. Again, being effective requires knowing what you want and choosing the behaviors that most align with your goal.

In mindfulness, you practice one "what" skill with all of the "how" skills. For example, you may observe the flowers in your garden in a way that is fully present and non-judgmental, aligned with your goal of taking a mindful moment.

I have already discussed the general benefits of mindfulness. But I'd like to get a little more specific about the superpower that is cultivated specifically from practicing mindfulness. First, mindfulness helps us to notice our experience without adding suffering to pain. Remember that when we place judgments on an experience, we can prolong the pain and create suffering. Either we make pain worse, when we reject negative experiences, or we lessen joy because we are so attached and wish that the feeling will last forever. Even positive judgements, like "I am worthy," are tricky because being worthy necessarily implies the possibility that we could be worthless. Second, mindfulness gets us out of autopilot and we learn to respond rather than react. Instead of immediately succumbing to an urge to fight or to use a substance, we give ourselves room to respond in a way that is "effective" toward our goals. As Viktor Frankl noted, between stimulus and response, there is a space in which we can freely choose our actions. I believe mindfulness allows us to be much more attuned to this space and gives us the power to act in accordance with our values.

At a mental health and addictions research clinic, I applied mindfulness-based practices to support relapse prevention for folks who struggled with substance use. There was a research component which involved the use of virtual reality in the mindfulness practice. It was pretty cool to use advanced technology to really bring the meditations to life. The patients would put on the headgear and then be virtually transported to the top of a mountain during the practice. Again, the point of the mindfulness practice was to cultivate an awareness of the present moment and practice stepping out of autopilot. This practice helped cultivate space for the patient to notice their cravings to substances and learn to respond rather than react.

The intention of mindfulness, whether sitting on a mountain created by virtual reality or taking a walk, is simply to bring awareness to the present moment. When practicing mindfulness, some of my patients say that the practice did not help them. The question I ask in return is "help with what?" The reason I ask this question is because people turn to mindfulness with the intention of feeling happier, becoming less anxious, and getting rid of unpleasant experiences. However, that is not the point of mindfulness. Mindfulness is about simply attending to the very moment. Whether our mind is quiet as a lake or as chaotic as a thunderstorm, whether we are at complete peace or total discomfort, we simply allow our experience to be just as it is. There is no right or wrong way to practice mindfulness. If you are doing your best to stay present-focused and non-judgmental, then you are being mindful.

I also try to incorporate mindfulness in my life and throw myself in the moment. Even in situations where I feel very anxious and uncomfortable, I lean into the experience. There's a lot of beauty that comes from being willing to be in the moment, whether it's sitting underneath the sunshine or allowing yourself to be right in the eye of the emotional storm. I'll say it again. There is no right way to practice mindfulness. Even at this moment, if you are fully engaged in the reading of this book, then that is mindfulness. And if not, then your awareness of this fact and intentional refocusing on the words, is mindfulness.

Like most skills, I think of mindfulness like a muscle. It takes consistent practice to apply mindfulness into our lives. People believe that they are bad at mindfulness because they feel uncomfortable or their mind is incessant with random thoughts. But it's okay. You have full permission to be uncomfortable and your mind has full permission to wander. That is what minds do after all. Whenever this happens, simply notice what thoughts carried you away and return to the present moment. Welcome back.

10

The Power of Paradoxical Intention

"Like they say in Zen, when you attain Satori, nothing is left to you at that moment but to have a good laugh."—
Alan Watts

Life can be a curious paradox. When we try to force something to happen, like falling in love, then love is nowhere to be found. It is when we least expect romance that love seems to be right around the corner. It is the law of reversed effort: The more we want something, the further away it seems to get. This principle can be found in love, sleep, and even stability—the more we force certainty into an ever-changing world, the less stable we become. Yet when we let go and join the dance of life, that is when we paradoxically cultivate a sense of stability. Thus, the lesson that arises from this paradox is that sometimes we need to lean into our fears to achieve certain outcomes. To embrace love, we must be comfortable being alone. To obtain sleep, we must be willing to be awake. To feel a sense of stability, we must be willing to leap into an uncertain world.

I also lean into my own fears when working with patients. In dialectical behavior therapy, there is a concept known as "treading where angels fear to tread." People with borderline personality disorder often present with significant suicidality. Therapists reasonably worry about the patient killing themselves and begin tiptoeing around them in fear of triggering an emotional response. However, these behaviors only remind them of the same way that everybody else in their life treats them. Instead, I dare to tread where angels fear and lean into the discomfort. In response to threats of suicide, I may take a matter-of-fact approach and say something like: "If you keep talking about killing yourself, I can't be helpful to you. The ethics protocol requires me to assess for risk and I may need to call emergency services. This will be another horrible therapy experience for you and I won't be the effective therapist that you need." This willingness to dive into the lion's cave and come from a place of resilience rather than fragility, can often be quite refreshing for patients. I have found that being willing to treat the patient as though they were a strong person rather than handling them in a delicate manner can cultivate a sense of strength and well-being. This approach is similar to the Pygmalion effect where higher expectations can lead to improved performance.

The willingness to tread where angels fear to tread can also be applied to other mental health concerns. In panic disorder, people treat their panic symptoms as seriously as a heart attack. I mean this figuratively, but also in a literal sense. People with panic disorder worry that their anxiety symptoms are a sign of a life-threatening condition. A wise therapist recognizes that panic symptoms are not inherently dangerous and will work with the patient to better tolerate these uncomfortable sensations. Most evidence-based providers will typically apply a gradual exposure protocol. They will build out an exposure hierarchy and pick a practice that is challenging but manageable. For example, jogging in place for thirty seconds to elicit symptoms of shortness of breath and racing heart. While I think this approach is absolutely reasonable and effective (and probably where I would go too), I believe we can lean into the fear of a heart attack in the spirit of the law of reversed effort. When we are doing a gradual exposure practice, we are treating the symptoms rather seriously. We are essentially admitting to the patient and ourselves that facing our panic symptoms is a fearful practice and we need to take a gradual approach to avoid being overwhelmed. I wonder if there is a way to see the experience as something wholly distinct and take an exaggerated, light-hearted approach to these symptoms of panic.

At the core of these musings is a practice called paradoxical intention. The underlying idea behind paradoxical intention is that people experience something called anticipatory anxiety. We get anxious when we think about confronting a scary situation, which can lead to the feared outcome being more likely to happen. For example, if we are nervous about being able to stay aroused during sexual intercourse, then the anxiety will lead to that worry coming true. From an insomnia perspective, our fear of not being able to sleep becomes the catalyst for another restless night. The goal of paradoxical intention then is to stare at the feared outcome straight in the eye and fully embrace the fear. In doing so, we may come to realize that the fear runs a mile wide but an inch deep.

In the context of panic disorder, we may leap into our fear by saying to ourselves: "You know what? My heart isn't racing nearly enough to have a heart attack! Let me run even faster to see if I can actually go into cardiac arrest." In the case of insomnia disorder, we work to reduce our fear of not falling asleep by embracing the idea of being fully awake at night. In fact, I will sometimes ask the patient to pick a day where they lie in bed and get them to try to stay awake all night. Unsurprisingly, patients have a hard time staying awake when they have given themselves permission to stop trying to force sleep to happen. This is because the patient no longer feels pressured to sleep which reduces performance anxiety.

Let's also take an example in obsessive compulsive disorder and obsessions related to contamination. Generally, folks with contamination obsessions will be hyper-sensitive to touching anything that they perceive to be dirty or diseased. In paradoxical intention, the goal would be to touch anything and everything. Your goal is to be as contaminated as possible and collect all the germs and dirt like you would Pokémon cards. Besides contamination, I once had a patient named Alex who struggled with obsessive worries about being a bad person and wanting to hurt other people. Alex would constantly have images flash in his mind about strangling people. Out of a moralistic worry that these images meant he truly wanted to hurt other people, Alex would feel distress whenever these violent images popped up in his mind. Unfortunately, this concern only increased the frequency of these intrusive images. We were making some progress with the usual treatment strategies of exposure practice to tolerate distress and cognitive therapy to challenge his beliefs about being a bad person. However, the improvement was slow and arduous. I considered paradoxical intention as a possible intervention and I encouraged Alex to spend the next week leaning into his worries about hurting other people. I asked him to imagine himself as Godzilla firing out atomic breaths into the city. He was understandably a little nervous about the idea but it certainly gave him a good laugh.

Paradoxical intention is easier said than done. There's a reason why we experience anticipatory anxiety. We are attached to the outcome. If we could truly embody the perspective of not caring, there would be no anxiety in the first place. The problem is that we feel fused with the experience and it is hard to let go of something that seems so important in the moment. Therefore, we require something that helps with taking perspective with our problems. I think that the missing piece that we are looking for is humor. Humor is an incredible power that allows us to experience something in a completely different light. For example, being able to laugh at myself and say "Wow, I can be a terrible student sometimes!" demonstrates an ability to separate the "self" from the experience. It's kind of like being on top of a mountain and observing ourselves from a third-person perspective. We can laugh with the wisdom that our experience is meaningful and meaningless at the same time. And that regardless of what happens, we are going to be okay. Humor is a very mindful practice if you think about it. When you are laughing, you are not in the future nor in the past, you are right here in the moment. The next time you feel like the world is going to end and there's nothing you can do about it, I encourage you to have a good laugh—and then leap right into this wonderful and bizarre experience known as life.

11

The Dance of Yin and Yang

"I am because you are."—Zulu proverb

There is a sort of disharmony in opposite experiences. The existence of one implies the negation of the other. We may even come to see the existence of other people as threats to our own selves. The light in other people casts a shadow onto mine. Their success is my failure; their intelligence reveals my incompetence; and their uniqueness makes me painfully ordinary. Even in our daily life, we constantly evaluate our experiences and separate them as good or bad. The pain in my stomach is horrible. The grade I received on my organic chemistry exam is stellar. The argument I had with my partner last night was miserable. The weather is terrible. Every part of existence is binned into categories by the judge in our minds. We desire to only experience the good parts of life and do our best to avoid the bad. We want to always be happy and never sad, to succeed and not fail, and to be healthy for the rest of our lives. Unsurprisingly, the market for leading happy, healthy, and successful lives is perennially popular. There are any number of gurus with their podcasts that teach us the perfect protocol to optimize every part of our waking and sleeping lives, fitness channels that promise to sculpt our bodies into Greek statues, and self-help books (like this one) that teaches us how to live happily and with purpose. We also have individuals like Bryan Johnson treating themselves as a science experiment to learn the secrets to immortality and arrest the aging process. We view negative experiences, such as sadness, loneliness, sickness, and death as something mutually exclusive from its counterpart. To be sad means that I am missing out on times when I could be happy. To be sick means that I lose out on the gift of good health. Death is the enemy of life. It certainly makes me wonder: Is there a way to stop denying half of existence? Can we make sense and meaning of the experiences that seem to get in the way of the perfect life.

If you remember Andy, he was a patient of mine who had recently started a new job at an investment firm. This was a huge milestone in terms of his career goals, something that he had been working toward for a long time. Andy had made a commitment early in his life to prioritize his career in order to financially secure his future. He therefore spent most of his school days in the library and he now spends the majority of his time dedicated to his career. Although his investments had paid dividends toward his long-term goal, in our sessions, Andy reflected that he was having second thoughts about whether this type of high-powered, time-consuming career was truly the mountain he wanted to climb. He had candid conversations with his work seniors about their experiences in their field. And despite being several years further along in their career, Andy realized that these peoples' lives still continued to heavily revolve around work. In fact, their work-life balance was even more heavily skewed toward the work side. And Andy already worked pretty hard; he would generally spend at least 70 to 80 hours a week at work.

His seniors continued to place work above everything else. However, Andy wasn't sure he wanted to follow in their footsteps. He realized that his values had shifted over the years, and he wanted to have work integrated into his life, not dominated by it. He enjoyed spending time with his girlfriend, going to the gym, and playing basketball on the weekends with his friends. However, work often competed against these values. Given the demands of his job, Andy worked well into the evenings on weekdays and often took meetings on weekends. Even when he was off the clock, Andy was still constantly ruminating about work and his performance in his new role.

Andy was somewhat melancholic about this realization that he didn't want his career to be the centerpiece of his life. He was fraught with regret that he had spent so much of his youth focusing on work just to veer off course so far into the journey. He also felt like straying this path would be betraying his younger self and the intense amount of work and sacrifice it took for him to get to his current position. If he had known his values would shift so greatly, he may have chosen a different path from the beginning.

Andy's past and present values felt like enemies. There was no room for both and the price of accepting one would be at the cost of invalidating the other. Therefore, reconciliation seemed impossible. Because I knew that this push-pull was creating inner conflict for Andy, we discussed ways to see whether we could make harmony of these seemingly mutually exclusive paths. I wondered out loud that perhaps Andy would have never realized his current values without his past experiences. That is, without having spent so many years focusing on climbing the mountain, that he would have never had the perspective of what truly mattered to him in the present moment. It was only through the road paved with his hard work that Andy could look at his life from a different vantage point. If he had never prioritized his work to this extent, then maybe he would still be thinking that an illustrious career was his ultimate goal.

This reflection was a helpful reframe for Andy. He hadn't considered that he may not have come to the conclusion about what truly mattered if he didn't put in the initial effort to work hard and focus on his career. He was still in an excellent position to leverage his current financial situation to take care of his family, which was an important value. At the same time, Andy could start to also refocus from work toward building his relationships and spending time on enjoyable hobbies. From this, Andy was able to reconcile his current values with his past actions and thank his past self for his hard work. This reframing allowed him to integrate his experiences into a more cohesive narrative. That without one, there could not be the other.

One of the ideas I really find beautiful from Andy's story is that people can create harmony from seemingly competing ideas and experiences. In fact, perhaps only through experiencing one can we truly know the other. There is a profound gratitude that comes from honoring such a perspective. It is only when I am sick as a dog that I can truly appreciate what it means to be in good health. From experiencing the shivering cold of winter, I can fully delight in the warm embrace of spring. Through the pain of sadness, I can know the pleasure of happiness. There is a quote from American painter Bob Ross that I think wonderfully captures the heart of this idea. Shortly after his wife Jane passed away of cancer in 1992, Ross would share his wisdom to his audience in his show *The Joy of Painting*: "Gotta have opposites, light and dark and dark and light, in painting. It's like in life. Gotta have a little sadness once in a while so you know when the good times come. I'm waiting on the good times now." In art, dark and light are essential to create a sense of depth to bring the artwork to life. Without dark, the painting would look bland and uninspired. Similarly, different experiences, some more painful than others, dance in harmony together to create life's vibrant and dynamic tapestry.

I find that this gratitude can even extend toward the fact that we are also defined in relation to other people. For example, if everyone around me was as fast as Usain Bolt, compassionate as Mother Teresa, or a total Einstein, it would be pretty challenging to consider myself as being kind or smart. Perhaps you are considered the considerate one in the group because your friends tend to be a little less careful. It may be that other people are more social that you are thought of as more introverted. We rely on each other to exist and be our imperfectly perfect selves.

As a therapist, I've certainly had patients that were challenging, who were frustrated and sometimes treated me less than kindly, and I would feel impatient or irritated in turn. However, I understood that these patients were struggling with their mental health and came to me for support. They needed a therapist. And it is precisely because of the patient in front of me that I can be the person who gives support. When I take this frame, I become profoundly appreciative of the person in front of me. I can only be helpful when there is someone who needs help. I can only be a therapist when there is a patient. I can only be a writer when there is a reader. I am because you are.

This way of thinking was also helpful for a patient of mine named Max, who struggled with existential concerns about death. For Max, the idea of death had scared him since he was an elementary school student when his grandmother passed away. His death anxiety permeated in his life and made him feel compelled to constantly think of ways to live life to the fullest. Consequently, when he had a bad day, because of headaches or sickness, it created a lot of distress. These experiences made him feel like he was wasting the gift of life. Max felt that life was short, and the bad days further reduced his ability to make the most of his precious time on the planet.

Of course, it's normal to *prefer* a good day. However, Max felt like he needed every day to be good. As a result, this served to increase his distress when something impacted his ability to fully enjoy the day. In some ways, this fear of having a bad day was also a self-fulfilling prophecy. As Steven Hayes, the founder of acceptance of commitment therapy once said: "If you aren't willing to have it, you will." Whenever Max noticed that he was having a rough start to the day, that would lead him to start focusing only on the negatives. He would ruminate about how his day wasn't going as planned, which increased his distress and made him decide to just stay home and do nothing.

Max and I talked about how good and bad days are not necessarily enemies. The existence of good days implies the existence of bad days and without one you don't have the other. We also tried to find harmony in the ideas of life and death. Together, we considered a thought experiment and I asked Max what he thought life would be like if he were to live forever. He responded that it would probably feel pretty tortuous after a while. Max also doubted that he would feel very motivated to focus on his goals knowing that there was no time limit and, in some ways, no point. Death therefore gave life meaning. Irvin Yalom once proclaimed that "though the physicality of death destroys us, the idea of death may save us."

I won't pretend that through our discussions Max suddenly started jumping for joy the next time he was sick or that his 2:00 a.m. existential dread suddenly disappeared. I also won't pretend that I am never frustrated at work or that I find great pleasure in a patient complaining about me not being of any help. But I think this perspective offers some solace when dealing with painful experiences by understanding their place in our lives rather than rejecting them. I invite you to think about negative experiences a little differently, even if just not to let momentary pain turn into prolonged suffering. Try to acknowledge and accept painful experience as part of the broader tapestry of life—something that makes life brim with depth and vibrancy. This perspective doesn't mean you simply accept all the bad things into your life. If the problem is solvable then solve it. At the same time, this perspective is a reminder that trying to avoid painful experiences only invites more pain and prolongs it. If you are a little delusional like me, you might even find joy and meaning no matter where you are in the yin and yang of life.

12

Making Friends with Your Emotions

"Crying helps me slow down and obsess over the weight of life's problems."—Sadness in *Inside Out*

The cognitive behavioral model has a diagram that contains three boxes with arrows that point to each other. These boxes are labelled thoughts, behaviors, and emotions. Clinicians present this diagram to patients in order to illustrate that how we think, behave, and feel are all interconnected and mutually influence each other. However, not all components are treated equally. CBT clinicians in particular tend to spend most of therapy focusing on just the behaviors and cognitions leaving poor old emotion high and out to dry. The only crumb that emotion tends to get is its role as a quick assessment check to see if a person feels differently after using the cognitive and behavioral strategies. Unfortunately, this lack of emphasis on emotions can leave a lot of clinical gains on the table. A common issue that I hear with patients in cognitive therapy is "I understand it logically, but I don't *feel* it." Therefore, if the ideas do not resonate with the patient emotionally, then they cannot truly connect with the lessons no matter how good they sound in theory.

There are significant merits to focusing on emotions in therapy. Even just the act of naming an emotional experience can be therapeutic and show the patient that someone truly understands their internal world. Labelling one's emotions, such as saying "I feel sad" or "I am ashamed" also has a powerful downregulating effect. That is, the act of recognizing and naming what we are feeling can take the edge off the emotion and foster a sense of well-being. Moreover, when emotions are less intense, we are more readily able to apply skills to manage emotions and work effectively toward our goals. If we can admit to ourselves that we feel upset or guilty about a situation, then we can face reality and focus on the most helpful behaviors. There are no shortage of reasons to bring in the third musketeer into therapy. The lesson is simple: Changing our relationship with emotions can have a profound impact in how we operate in our lives.

There are some therapies, like dialectical behavior therapy, that conceptualize problem behaviors as reactions to distressing emotions. For example, some folks are very averse to negative emotions, like shame and guilt, and cope with them by drowning them with alcohol or through mindlessly scrolling on social media. Other people may repress the emotions, kind of like how Joy in *Inside Out 2* catapulted spheres representing bad experiences into the abyss. This "out of sight, out of mind" approach works in the short-term; however, the emotions do not just simply disappear. They will eventually bubble their way back into the surface. Over time, these repressed emotions will act like straws on a camel's back and will weigh on us until the inevitable emotional avalanche crushes everything in its wake. Another example of unhelpful coping is to cover up the more vulnerable emotion with a "secondary" emotion. A secondary emotion is the emotion in response to the primary emotion. For example, we may hide our feelings of shame through anger. One of my patients Sandi had a troubled childhood and was constantly criticized by her parents. As a result, she came to expect the same judgment from other people, especially in places where she felt particularly vulnerable. In the group therapy room, Sandi worried that other members were annoyed about the fact that she was talking too much or that they would notice she was fidgety and wonder what the heck was wrong with her. These fears led to a lot of shame and anxiety. To shield herself from these hurtful emotions, Sandi would cover them up with a flash of anger and start throwing out her own judgments: "How dare they judge me and make me feel this way? They are all way crazier than I am!" The secondary emotion of anger was a response to her primary emotions of shame. Although the anger worked to protect her from more painful emotions and wrestle back a sense of control, this unwillingness to sit with her vulnerability negatively impacted her ability to engage in group treatment and bond with the other participants.

The above coping strategies work to tuck our emotions away and hope they don't come back to bite us in the rear. There are some folks that deal with the opposite problem and have a hard time managing the intensity of their emotions. Their sadness feels like absolute agony and their anger makes even the devil's blood run cold. The urge to follow what the emotion is telling them to do becomes irresistible. Prolonged sadness leads to folks fully withdrawing from life for months on end; unbridled anger may burn bridges with friends and family; and crushing anxiety paralyzes us from moving toward our goals. The way that people deal with challenging emotions can therefore vary from those who fully disconnect from them to those who feel like they are squarely in the eye of the emotional storm. Consequently, it's important to identify where we are in this teeter-totter of emotional experiences to bring balance into our lives.

We treat emotions, especially the painful ones, as though they are our enemies and need to be controlled. However, emotions do not have to be tamed like wild beasts. Even the most uncomfortable emotions come with a lot of wisdom if we can learn to sit with them and hear what they are saying. Sadness tells us that we have lost something important; guilt tells us that we have done something that we believe is wrong; happiness tells us that we are doing something that is personally meaningful to us; anger tells us that one of our boundaries have been crossed; and fear tells us that there is a threat nearby. When we ignore these messages, we risk feeling invalidated. For example, we may feel rightfully angry that a friend is taking advantage of us or be appropriately nervous about an upcoming qualifying exam for licensure in our profession. In this case, we can resolve these emotions through actions such as setting boundaries or properly preparing for the exam.

It is therefore important to identify the emotion we are

experiencing in the moment and then determine whether the emotion fits the facts of the situation. In cases where the emotion absolutely fits the facts, like the anxiety that comes from being next to a sleeping bear, then it would be helpful to follow what the anxiety is telling us and escape from the bear-infested area. Other instances include listening to the guilt and apologizing when you have done something wrong or accepting the feelings of anger and setting a boundary when an in-law has been constantly unfair to you.

However, there are also cases where the emotions do not fit the facts. Perhaps you feel a lot of anxiety about making mistakes when drafting emails. However, it is rare for you to make any errors. Moreover, any typos or omissions you have made in the past have never led to any significant problems. In this case, the anxiety does not fit the facts. It would then be important to act opposite to what the emotion is telling you to do and avoid checking too many times. There are also times where the emotions fit the facts, but it may not be helpful to follow the urge associated with the emotion. For example, sadness might tell us to withdraw from the world and stop engaging in activities that used to give us joy and meaning. Although taking some time to process sadness can absolutely be helpful, if we stop engaging with the world for prolonged periods of time, then the sadness can turn into chronic depression. Therefore, we need to eventually start re-engaging with the world even if there is a good reason why we are feeling sad. In this case, we are honoring the truth of the emotion while simultaneously leaning into the idea of being effective in pursuit of our goals.

Changing our relationship with emotions is not easy. My emotions and I are not always the best of friends, and I find myself a bit more on the overregulated side. My emotional range tends to fluctuate from mildly displeased to reasonably content. My elementary school principal (who also moonlighted as our badminton coach) once compared me to a stone. That is, I had about as much expression on my face as the moai on Easter Island. From very young, I definitely leaned more toward the reserved side. I suspect my desire to hold back emotions stemmed from feeling socially anxious and not wanting to draw too much attention to myself by keeping composure at all times. However, these types of coping behaviors backfire, as they typically do, and people would ironically take more notice of me because of my unusual stiffness.

In some cases, I have noticed this relative lack in emotional range to be viewed positively by other people. They might describe me as even keeled and a source of comfort since I keep so composed in stressful situations. Though, I don't think of my demeanor as the big "S" Stoic like Marcus Aurelius or Epictetus. This would suggest a healthy relationship with emotions where emotions are well-managed through reason and self-discipline. Rather, I see my relationship as the small "s" stoic where I am suppressing them and not actually dealing with the "bad" emotions. The problem with this management strategy is I don't know how to handle big emotions when they inevitably float to the surface. I find myself occasionally passive aggressive much to the chagrin of my wife (very sorry!) because I don't know how to sit with anger and express my boundaries clearly. I also notice it hard to be vulnerable and sit with sadness, which would be helpful to properly process emotions rather than feeling like a shaken Pepsi bottle where the air has nowhere to escape.

In my case, I'd do well with practicing exposing myself to more emotions. To sit with Sadness for a moment and obsess over the weight of life's problems or hang out with Anger and let him guide me in standing up for myself. Remember, the goal of this practice is not to get rid of uncomfortable emotions. It's about not prolonging them any more than necessary and not turning pain into suffering. Sadness can be painful no doubt. However, if we can sit with the emotion and allow it to be present in our lives, then we can process our reasons for feeling sad and then let sadness go when it is ready. If we reject what sadness is telling us, then the feeling will continue to linger with us and slowly turn into suffering. This practice of sitting with our emotions can even be helpful even with emotions that seem threatening or dangerous like anxiety. We can learn to sit with our anxiety and realize that it is not a harmful emotion. In fact, anxiety serves a useful function in protecting us. Over time, once you and anxiety have become a little closer as friends, perhaps you can even thank the emotion for alerting you of possible dangers in the environment.

If you recall, Avery was a patient who struggled with the feeling of "not-knowing." Avery would feel ashamed whenever they didn't understand a concept immediately and didn't know how to complete an assignment. Every time these feelings reared their ugly heads, Avery would turn away from these emotions by distracting themselves through social media. The problem was that this avoidance would lead to them falling further behind in their classes, which only exacerbated Avery's feelings of shame. Therefore, Avery and I came up with exposures to sit with these uncomfortable emotions. As a unique way of practicing this exposure, I set a prompt for ChatGPT to create a bunch of legal jargon and we both sat in front of the computer and read the AI generated passages. Given that few people outside of Harvey Specter and Mike Ross would be able to unravel these legal hieroglyphics, this exposure instigated that same feeling of not-knowing. Avery and I both sat with feelings of distress looking at the foreign passages. Over time, Avery noticed that their shame and anxiety began to reduce to more tolerable levels. Without the constant hum of these distressing emotions, Avery was better able to focus on the text and ended up understanding more than they thought!

There are also several strategies to manage the intensity of emotions to act more effectively in hard situations. If you recall, I briefly discussed in the first chapter that emotions, which seem like a single event, have many moving parts that comprise the experience. Changing one part of the experience can impact the whole system. In dialectical behavior therapy, there is a "model of emotions" which breaks down an emotional experience into ten parts: (1) the prompting event (i.e., the situation that causes the emotion), (2) attention/awareness, (3) interpretation of the event, (4) vulnerability factors, (5) biological changes (e.g., heart rate, temperature), (6) experiences (urges, body sensations), (7) expressions (facial expressions, actions), (8) emotion name, (9) aftereffects, and (10) secondary emotions. Let's break these parts down through an example:

In the evening, Jim and Pam are getting ready for dinner. During the dinner, Pam makes a comment that Jim has been working a lot recently and their daughter has been feeling lonely (prompting event). Jim notices the slight disappointment in Pam's voice (attention/awareness) and thinks that her comment suggested that he was not being a good dad (interpretation). Jim has been working a lot recently to build his company which has been quite stressful (vulnerability factor). In response to Pam's comment, Jim's heart starts beating harder (biological changes), his shoulder tightens and he has an urge to defend himself (experiences). Jim frowns and furrows his eyebrows and makes a sarcastic comment about certainly having hours every day to spend with them despite the fact that he is trying to build his company and provide for his family (expressions). At this point, Jim recognizes that he is quite angry about the comment and stays prickly the rest of the evening (aftereffects). He later feels shame for being angry and snapping at Pam (secondary emotion).

Remember that if you change one part, you can change the whole system. You can flexibly decide which of the different parts that make up an emotional experience would make the best sense to target. In some cases, avoiding the prompting event can be helpful. In the wise words of Mr. Miyagi, sometimes the best way to handle problems is to "no be there." For example, if there is a family member that tries to start arguments with you every time you see them, then it may be best to simply avoid spending time with them. However, in the case of Jim and Pam, this strategy may not be the most helpful in their situation. Other strategies include using distracting strategies to take our attention away from something causing us grief, changing our interpretation of the event (e.g., "Pam is probably just feeling lonely and does not mean to suggest that I am being a bad husband or father"), or nourishing ourselves to reduce vulnerability by doing things that are healthy and enjoyable. Biological experiences like heart palpitations could be managed through relaxation exercises. A particularly helpful strategy is the use of "opposite to emotion action" to compete with action urges. For example, this can include smiling when we are sad or being kind to others even when we are angry. The act of naming the emotion can have a powerful effect to reduce its intensity. The wonderful part of these skills is that any of them can work to shift the balance of the system, so you can decide based on the situation, your goals, and what feels right for you.

Ultimately, the question of where you are with your relationship with your emotion will guide the answer of how to best relate to them differently. Can you listen to the wisdom of your emotion? Are you able to sit with them and hear what they are saying without feeling overwhelmed? Can you identify the primary emotion? For example, perhaps Jim's anger was really a secondary emotion to the primary emotion of sadness thinking that Pam believed he wasn't there for his family. In some cases, you may need to give permission for the emotions to rise up and sit with the raw vulnerability. Other times you will have to manage them properly in order to act effectively in the situation. Your emotions are not enemies; rather, they are your friends doing their best to support you. Sometimes, they might jump the gun and be a little too eager to help out. Other times, they may worry about hurting you and stay quiet. I invite you to try and make friends with your emotions. To sit with them for a little while and listen to their wisdom.

13

Filling Your Cup

"The first wealth is health."—Ralph Waldo Emerson

For just a moment, I invite you to imagine a particularly tough day. You had an argument with your partner last night. Ruminating over the argument, you did not get much sleep. You were tossing and turning all night in the fuzzy twilight zone between sleep and wake. Unfortunately, you can't sleep in because you have to wake up early for work. Because of morning mishaps and unfortunate red lights, you are half an hour late for work. You are hungry, thirsty, and tired. And you want nothing more than to hide away in your room and decompress. However, you are a responsible adult and have to put on a smiling face for those around you. You try your best, but there is a small part of you that is acutely aware that if any customer decides to push their luck today, you would be willing to step into mutually assured destruction territory.

When we feel depleted, even small annoyances can push us over the edge of insanity. It becomes increasingly difficult to manage life stressors. Therefore, we need to be mindful of the activities that nourish and deplete us to support our emotion regulation. There are three components to emotion regulation, which is our ability to manage emotions effectively on a daily basis: baseline, reactivity, and recovery. We can think of our emotional baseline as how we feel on a day to day. Some of us may feel generally grounded whereas others walk around with a slight chip on their shoulders. When a stressor occurs, like somebody cutting in front of us while we are waiting in line, we experience a reactive shift in our emotions. Following the stressor, we take some time in the recovery period until we return to our baseline.

There are evidence-informed strategies that can help manage our emotional response to stress and hasten recovery to baseline. For example, these include the use of mindfulness and emotion regulation skills, such as deep breathing, intense exercise, or splashing our face with cold water. In the spirit of Benjamin Franklin's proclamation that "an ounce of prevention is worth a pound in cure," if we can reduce our emotional vulnerability, then we can better handle whatever life throws at us before it even happens. An analogy for reducing emotional vulnerability is like filling your cup. A content baseline means that your cup is nicely filled. When life starts to hand you lemons, then you have a well-filled cup to pour out the fires of your life. However, if you are feeling depleted and your cup is empty, then you won't be able to readily deal with them. It'll take much longer and be more painful to finally pat dry.

Activities can be broadly categorized into being nourishing or depleting. Nourishing activities fill our cup and depleting activities drain our cup. The specific impact that activities have on our emotional wellsprings will depend on the person. For example, people who are more on the extroverted side may find socializing to be nourishing, whereas introverts may find social interactions to drain their cup. Some social relationships may also be more meaningful and nourishing than others, such as the difference between having a coffee catch-up with an old friend versus making uncomfortable chitchat in an elevator.

There are some broader principles that we can rely on to add nourishing activities into our lives. There is a cute acronym in dialectical behavior therapy called ABC PLEASE. The ABC stands for accumulate positives, build mastery, and cope ahead. Accumulate positives means finding things, big or small, in your life that fosters pleasant feelings. This could include listening to your favorite passage of a song on repeat, treating yourself to a fun Starbucks drink, doing something kind for a stranger, reminiscing about being a child enjoying endless summers reading Harry Potter or playing

RuneScape, or sending some well-wishes to a loved one. Anything can work. I see accumulating positives like building out your own army of positive soldiers as a defense against the waves of stress for the future. It's kind of like assembling your own Avengers team of positivity.

The B in ABC stands for build mastery. Beyond simple pleasures, you are incorporating activities in your life that develop your sense of confidence and sense of resilience. If you feel a sense of self-efficacy, it becomes much harder for life's challenges to shake you. You simply feel more ready to deal with them. Just like accumulating positives, there are various ways to build mastery: learn a new language, practice an instrument, clean up your room, or study for an upcoming exam. Competence builds confidence because you obtain evidence that substantiates your sense of self-esteem. Look to start small and then engage in progressive overload—a fancy term common in bodybuilding to add more weight or repetitions to your workout as your body becomes stronger. In other areas of your life, progressive overload could be adding more vocabulary while learning languages, playing more challenging songs on the piano, or running for longer periods of time.

The C in ABC stands for cope ahead. It can be particularly hard to handle life's lemons when we are caught with our pants down. Coping ahead allows us to make sure that our pants are well-buckled before life comes at us. For example, one of my patients who was in the menopause transition struggled with hot flashes and night sweats in the middle of the night. These experiences would make it hard for her to fall back asleep. To cope ahead, we discussed keeping a glass of cold water and a change of clothing on her nightstand. These strategies wouldn't eliminate the uncomfortable symptoms, but it reduced the intensity of the stressor on her night and helped her to fall back asleep a little quicker. Similarly, I would encourage you to cope ahead if there are upcoming stressors in your life. For example, perhaps there is a meeting with the in-laws or a particularly busy day at work that would benefit from the cope ahead strategy.

The final part of this acronym is PLEASE. This is an especially silly acronym. It stands for treating physical illness, balanced eating, avoiding mood altering substances, balanced sleep, and getting exercise. If you are in the mood for some detective work, you can try to guess where the letters come from. Of course, the idea is not necessarily to overwhelm your life by optimizing every area. However, if there are certain components of the PLEASE skill that resonate with your goals, then start there.

While we're on the topic of potentially adding too many activities, it is important to properly pace yourself. Too many activities can also be depleting. We can think of fatigue as a homeostatic process, which means that there is an optimal amount of activity that maximizes energy and nourishment. Having too many or too few activities can negatively affect our well-being. I therefore think of energy like a generator rather than a battery. If we are doing nothing, then we have nothing to input into the generator. On the other hand, too much activity can overwhelm our generator and lead to overload. Therefore, I encourage you to give yourself a chance to take restful moments for yourself if you are the type of person that is always on the go.

Filling up your cup is an act of self-care. Some of you who are overly self-critical may find that you are your own worst enemy in taking time for yourself. After all, you can't help but try to fill up other people's cups first. However, if we were to play around with this analogy a little more, I think it is hard to fill up other people's cups when your own is empty. Instead, we need to take time to fill our own cup and then let the overflow fall into others. A thought that can come up is "I don't deserve it." This sort of negative self-judgment can make us less willing to engage in self-care. Rather than asking the question of whether you deserve care, I encourage you to ask a different question: "Will this be helpful?" This question removes judgment and only focuses on effectiveness. And the answer is likely yes, because filling your cup will naturally put you in a better position to help others.

Pema Chödrön, a Tibetan Buddhist once said that in order to give other people compassion, you must first provide compassion toward yourself. To this end, I invite you to end this session with a short loving-kindness meditation. Close your eyes, take a breath, and repeat to yourself: "May I be safe, may I be happy, maybe I be well, may I rest with ease." Then, I encourage you to extend these wishes to somebody in your life that is easy to love—a child, a pet, or somebody else. Finally, I invite you to expand these well-wishes into the world. And if this loving-kindness practice is a bit hard to practice right now, just know that when I wrote this passage, I was sending my own well-wishes. And I hope you were able to receive them.

14

Act First, Feel Second

"It's often easier to act yourself into feeling, than it is to think yourself into a new way of acting."—Millard Fuller

Rory was a kind and sociable 19-year-old who actively participated in her life. She was unique in her ability to find joy in the ordinary: watching hummingbirds flit between zinnias and columbines to drink their sweet nectar, smelling the freshly brewed coffee from her home Nespresso machine, and being entranced by the swaying of the trees as if they were a pleasant greeting from Mother Nature herself. In her daily life, Rory spent her days playing volleyball with her friends at her local YMCA and her evenings watching classic 90s flicks on Netflix. On the weekends, she volunteered at a senior center, and in the evenings, she was studying to be an athletic coach as part of her kinesiology degree.

Over the past year, Rory noticed that her daily life didn't give her the same pleasure and enjoyment as it did in the past. The colors in Rory's world had turned a little more grayscale. The birds and flowers had lost some pop in their colors and the trees' salutation was a little less captivating. Rory's world soon began to shrink. She reduced her days volunteering at the senior center. She made excuses to her friends about feeling too tired to play volleyball. She also found it hard to concentrate on her studies. Rory was still watching movies and scrolling on her phone, but it was out of boredom rather than interest. Rory didn't feel sad per se; she just felt "blah." The gravitational pull from the depression drew her onto the couch browsing through social media for endless hours. It was like the feeling of freedom and bounce in her step that used to be defining features of Rory was weighed down by a blanket of sadness.

Low mood and anhedonia—defined as the inability to take enjoyment or pleasure in the things that used to give us these feelings—are cardinal symptoms of depression. Cardinal means that at least one of these two symptoms are required for a diagnosis of major depression. Fundamentally, low mood and anhedonia make engaging in meaningful activities much less reinforcing. They just don't give us the same good feelings anymore. As a result, we gradually stop engaging in life because it all feels unenjoyable, unpleasant, and unrewarding for the amount of effort it takes to do them. Even getting out of bed can feel like climbing a mountain. The problem is that depression is a self-perpetuating disorder. The lack of positive reinforcement, the stuff that used to give us that joie de vivre, makes our depression even worse, which then negatively feeds back into engaging in even less activities. Simply put, we stop doing fun and meaningful things and depression continues to feed off the emptiness of our lives.

This elegant way of explaining how depression is maintained led to a very logical treatment of chronic low mood. If depression takes away the things that are most enjoyable and meaningful for us, then we need to start bringing them back. This idea forms the basis of an evidence-based treatment for depression known as behavioral activation. We can take full advantage of the fact that (1) we are resilient humans who can do hard things even when it is hard and (2) how we behave can influence how we feel (and not just the other way around). We often hold an implicit assumption that we need to feel something in order to do it. We need to be happy in order to smile or we need to feel confident in order to talk to a stranger. However, this "following a feeling" strategy does not work very well when we constantly feel depressed. After all, depression makes us want to do nothing. However, our behaviors can precede our emotions and even change them. For example, if we sit up with hands on our lap, palms facing up, and turn our frown upside down into a tiny half-smile, we may notice that we feel just a little bit more open and content. Not a huge amount, mind you. But just a little bit. And there's a lot of change that can happen with a little happiness.

In behavioral activation, there are five primary types of activities that can be important to reintegrate into patients' lives. These include activities of pleasure, mastery, connection, approach, and meaning. *Pleasure* activities include anything that is pleasant and enjoyable. This might include listening to music, enjoying a hot bath, or watching a rerun of *Friends*. *Mastery* activities are those that make us feel more competent, such as learning a new language, cleaning our room, or practicing an instrument. *Connection* activities are about social relationships: calling your best friend, visiting your family for Christmas, or going on a romantic date. *Approach* activities are tasks that we have been avoiding. For example, we approach when we make an important phone call, finish up a term paper, or apply for a new job. And finally, *meaning* activities are the ones that you personally value. What is meaningful will vary from person to person. And certainly, some activities will fall into multiple buckets. For example, playing in an orchestra could be something that contributes to pleasure, mastery, social connections, as well as meaning.

It is important to take stock of the different types of activities that depression or the busy-ness of life has taken away from you. Perhaps your life is still filled with pleasurable activities, but there has been a reduction in activities that foster mastery and self-esteem. For others, they could be forcing themselves to work and burn the midnight candle, but they may no longer participate in pleasurable activities or have started to withdraw from friends and family. In either case, the focus on behavioral activation is to bring back these cherished activities. Behavioral activation is not meant to be a mean-spirited treatment that simply forces you to do more for the sake of doing more. Behavioral activation instead tries to be a compassionate and patient-centered intervention that is mindful of each person's limited resources and directs these resources on the activities that will give them the biggest bang for their buck.

If you are unsure about what activities might be most helpful for you, it can be helpful to track your daily activities and how you feel when doing them. I used to run depression treatment groups at the Centre for Addiction and Mental Health in Toronto, Ontario. We would assign a practice called the mood-activity log. The task was that patients would write down what they were doing at different times of the day and rate their mood from a scale of 1 (absolutely terrible) to 10 (extremely happy) each hour. They would keep records for a week and bring it back next session for review. This was an insightful exercise because we could glean relationships between what the patient was doing and how they felt, which could inform ideas for scheduling activities using behavioral activation. It also allowed patients to reflect on what they have stopped doing since they started struggling with depression. Perhaps a person finds that they feel the happiest in meaningful social situations and realizes that they have stopped interacting as much with friends and family. The work would then focus on finding gradual ways to bring social connections back into this person's life. If this practice feels a little daunting, you can look for examples elsewhere to determine the activities that may resonate the most with you. For example, the American Psychological Academy has a "Pleasant Activities" list with over 200 common activities that people find enjoyable. The song "My Favorite Things" from *The Sound of Music* might also be another silly place to find inspiration for pleasurable activities.

Behavioral activation is simple in theory but can be challenging in practice. The strategy of acting first feeling second is tough when the pervasive feeling is one of chronic depression. You may also hold beliefs that this practice would be too hard or it won't help to improve how you feel. You might be right. At the same time, this thought is not particularly helpful and will only serve to keep you stuck in the depression trap. Like a curious scientist, I encourage you to treat behavioral activation as an experiment. It doesn't have to be a big experiment either. You can have a short phone call with a friend, treat yourself to an iced chai latte with vanilla cold foam, or sit in the park under the sun for a few minutes. My first patient Mike struggled with depression and a sense of hopelessness. He didn't think that anything could help him feel better. As a small experiment to see if certain activities could make him feel some joy, we used one of our therapy sessions to go on a walk to a nearby mall. And he did feel a little better. It was also a nice practice in behavioral activation for me too. I really enjoyed my chats with Mike during the walk and browsing books at Indigo with my first ever patient. So be curious, pick something you like, and give it a shot. After all, the best way to start is to start (small).

15

Time After Time

"Once you let your past decide how you experience the present, you have destroyed your future."—Sadhguru

A focus of psychodynamic therapy is exploring how past experiences affect our present. Well-known intrepid explorers of the psychodynamic unconscious include Carl Jung, Melanie Klein, Alfred Adler, and Sigmund Freud. Strategies that psychodynamic therapists use to delve into our innermost wishes and fears include free association, dream analysis, and Freudian slips (where you say one thing but mean your mother). The theory is that we typically do not have conscious access to what is driving our behaviors. Therefore, these techniques help us bring these unconscious processes into the surface. For example, in free association, people reflect on an issue in their life and allow themselves to say whatever comes to mind. A woman coming into therapy about relationship problems who is tasked to freely associate might come up with words like "stuck," "conflict," and "differences in values."

Dream analyses identify possible themes and derive meaning from these nighttime phenomena. A patient of mine would have nightmares nearly every night. One common nightmare included having arguments with her ex-husband. She would be trying to leave him in the dream but he would be screaming at her to stay in the relationship. In another nightmare, she would be watching an avalanche from a mountain above rapidly descending on her. She would get away in a car driven by her dad, but they would not be able to take everyone at the scene to safety. From her dreams, we identified common themes of safety and autonomy. The patient often felt very little control in her life. She felt like the plastic bag in Katy Perry's song "Firework" and felt helpless to deal with the stressors in her life. In this patient's case, she came to me for cognitive behavioral sleep treatment and not psychodynamic therapy. Consequently, we worked together to rescript her nightmares. Imagery rescripting is a strategy that is meant to change parts of the nightmare and we rehearse the new dream during the day. For example, the patient revised her avalanche nightmare such that she was able to drive everyone away to safety. To increase her sense of self-efficacy, I also tasked her to be the person to drive the car rather than her dad. The imagery rehearsal helped to reduce the frequency and intensity of her nightmares. Surprisingly, this practice even increased her own sense of self-control in her waking life too!

Today, the psychodynamic orientation—Freud specifically—has become less widespread in favor of mainstream treatments like cognitive behavioral therapy. Critics pooh-pooh many of Freud's claims because they cannot be tested using the scientific method. Moreover, there are certain ideas that are somewhat distasteful, such as Freud's psychosexual theory which place heavy emphasis on sexuality during development. Still it is undeniable that Sigmund Freud was a phenomenal thinker that generated significant momentum in the field of psychotherapy. A particularly important idea that continues to be useful in psychotherapy is the understanding that past experiences, especially during childhood, play a big role in the way we interact in the present world. For example, a woman may have constantly felt like she was a bother to other people. As a young child, her dad would ask her to go play with someone else because he was working and her mom would tell her to figure out problems herself. These early lessons become phantoms that then play out in present life. In this young woman's case, the early lessons learned was that she was not worthwhile and was not deserving of other people's time and effort. These traumatic lessons may express itself in therapy sessions, such as avoiding sharing vulnerable details to her therapist to not trouble them or trying to be extra considerate by always ending sessions right on time. She may also keep her emotional walls up even with her friends to avoid being perceived as too clingy or attached. In this chapter, we will start to make better sense of why we behave and think in certain ways. Through this understanding, we break the chains that tether us into the past, which permits us the freedom to determine our own future.

If you recall my patient Sandi, who struggled with anger in vulnerable situations, she was someone who considered herself stupid and worthless. As a child, her parents constantly made her feel dumb whenever she did not understand her schoolwork. Her father would beat her physically while shouting verbal insults. As a result, her "trauma network" activated whenever she thought other people were judging her performance. In those moments, she would revert back into that same powerless child being criticized by her parents. This sense of worthlessness would emerge even for daily tasks. For example, Sandi would feel incredibly ashamed when she did not know how to fill out certain sections of a form. She would then turn to distraction from the work. Although this strategy reduced her distress in the short-term, it also maintained her sense of incompetence in the long-term. Similarly, my other patient Avery and their parents made Avery feel that they were not a priority. Avery learned that their problems did not matter and subsequently stopped trying to get support from their family. Instead, Avery would start to dissociate whenever they noticed big feelings. As a child, they weren't capable of solving the problems and their parents were not of any help. Avery stopped looking toward their parents for support and instead burrowed inward to escape from the pain. It was best to simply tuck their problems away deep into the unconscious.

There are two issues that come from allowing the past to influence our present. The first is obvious: Our past is not our present. It may be true that early figures may have treated us like a hindrance. However, the people in our current life may actually cherish and value us. For Avery, this evidence of care came from when their friends had planned a surprise party for them. I reflected that this was rather powerful evidence that people in their life did care a lot. I joked that I've certainly rarely ever been on the receiving end of a surprise party. The second issue is that the strategies that may have worked well in the past may not be very helpful in the present moment. In Sandi's case, she typically got angry to make sure that other people would be less likely to be cruel toward her. However, this strategy may presently be a barrier to building meaningful relationships because other people would rightfully become afraid of her. Her anger therefore kept her from feeling vulnerable but also negatively impacted her ability to form strong positive relationships.

We can think of these mismatches in behavior and current context as a remnant of a past trauma being activated. When present situations remind us of past trauma, the same network in our brain comes online. In those moments, we feel like the same helpless child again. We then go into autopilot pulling for the same strategies that used to work. It is important to honor these behaviors and how they used to help us get through tough times. However, we must also recognize that these behaviors no longer serve the same useful function and they may now get in the way of our goals.

A very powerful clinical process to address these traumas that are playing out in the present moment is by calling attention to them within the therapeutic relationship. There is an idea used in psychodynamic therapy called transference. In therapy, patients will naturally start to bias their interactions with the therapist based on previous relationship dynamics. For example, a patient who has had past authority figures brush their concerns off might be particularly sensitive to invalidating actions. I like to follow my clinical Spidey senses when these "scripts" are being played out. I remember Sandi saying to me "I'll punch ya!" half-jokingly (we were on a video call) when I took a large inhale through my mouth. She was upset because she thought I was bored of her talking. I wasn't bored—my nose was just stuffy from allergies. However, her sensitivity to my potential boredom was informative. Together, we explored her worries about how she is being perceived by other people in different social contexts. As expected, Sandi's response to me was not an isolated experience. There were other times in her life when she would react aggressively when she felt other people were judging her. We identified that these aggressive responses stemmed from feelings of incompetence that were activated when it seemed like people didn't want to interact with her. This encounter allowed for a rich analysis that helped me better understand Sandi's experience in the real world. It also gave us space to figure out strategies to help Sandi manage these feelings of shame in a more effective manner. For example, we considered the use of distress tolerance strategies and sitting with shame rather than immediately acting aggressively.

Of course, therapy is a two-way street. Besides transference, there is another important piece to the therapeutic process known as countertransference, which is the therapist's own emotional reaction to the patient. With Sandi, I let her know that her occasional anger outbursts made me feel like I was walking on eggshells around her and found it hard to be my usual self. I also wondered aloud whether other people in her life might have a similar experience and be wary about getting too close. From this discussion we were able to help Sandi realize the impact of her interaction style on other people and support her toward more effective communication.

The insight to know when the trauma network is being activated can be useful. I often encourage patients to "check the facts" to decide whether their reaction in the moment makes sense in the present. For example, in Avery's case, their worries about being unloved was justified given their family history, but did not fit the facts in the present because of how much it seemed like their friends cared for them. As someone once wisely noted, if we do not learn from our history, we are doomed to repeat it. It is certainly very hard to not feel tethered by the past especially when we have experienced a history of traumatic invalidation. I invite you to see the world with a beginner's mind, as if you are experiencing it for the very first time without biases, preconceptions, or judgments. It takes courage to be vulnerable. But I believe in you. And so does Christopher Robin, who once said: "You're braver than you believe, stronger than you seem, and smarter than you think."

16

Everything Has Its Place

"I have cause. It is because I hate him."—Michael Scott from *The Office*

In Freudian psychoanalytic theory, there is a focus on etiology, which refers to understanding the cause of something. For example, let's say a child experienced an embarrassing situation in elementary school when the teacher called on them to answer a question about the history of Mesopotamia. In a moment of panic, the child froze and lost their ability to speak, and the only thing that came out was a high-pitched wheeze. The response was an eruption of laughter from classmates and a sigh of disappointment from the teacher. This formative experience might be one way etiology explains why the child later developed problems with social anxiety. Another big name in the psychodynamic space is Alfred Adler. His ideas are nicely captured in the book *The Courage to Be Disliked* by Fumitake Koga and Ichiro Kishimi. One important difference between Freud and Adler is that Adler's focus is not on the cause of a behavior, but rather *teleology*—the function behind the behavior. Teleology may explain that the person uses their social anxiety to protect themselves from future embarrassing situations. If the anxiety makes a person avoid risky social situations, then it is unlikely for them to experience another horrifying snafu. As we discussed with my patient Sandi, she generally turned to anger in situations where she felt vulnerable. From a teleological standpoint, the anger functioned to protect herself from feelings of shame and inferiority. She often worried about appearing stupid and being made fun of by others. Therefore, as a preventative measure, the anger worked to ensure that other people would not dare to criticize her—at least to her face.

For me, I tend to be rather introverted and spend more time listening than talking. If I were to analyze the function of my quietness from a teleological lens, I could see the purpose of this behavior to be seen as worthy. Deep down I think I come from a place of a general lack of self-esteem. Therefore, I participate minimally to increase my perceived sense of worth in two ways. The first from a place of scarcity, that things are more valuable in smaller quantities. I, consciously or unconsciously, believe that people may see my contributions as more insightful when I only sporadically offer my input. The second is that my few and far between contributions allow me to choose to participate only when I think I really have something worthwhile to say. Going with a sports analogy, I don't go up to bat unless I'm certain I can at least hit a double.

I suspect folks are following the idea of teleology rather well so far. But I think where Adler's perspective becomes less palatable is when it almost seems to "blame" the person for their circumstances. For example, Adler may go as far as to say that it is a teenager's choice to do poorly in school or a traumatized person's fault for not searching for a job. He may argue that the teenager performing poorly and causing disruptions in class are ways to obtain attention from his parents and teachers. If the teenager were to perform well, he would be treated just like any other student. It's kind of like how nobody notices the IT folks until the internet is down. In some ways, being disruptive was useful for the teenager to feel seen, and even negative attention is better than indifference. Similarly, Adler may explain that people choose not to find a job as a way to protect themselves from the fear of failure and rejection.

Some people regard this perspective as very invalidating and that nobody would choose to be in their situation. I feel the same way. At the same time, I acknowledge that sometimes the things that felt so rigid were more flexible than I thought. I remember my trip to Tokyo, which occurred over a decade ago now, and how I felt very free to shed my usual social chains. It was like I simply decided not to be tethered to what other people thought about me. I was not very worldly and had never been to Tokyo before. I knew barely a lick of Japanese. By all accounts, I should have been even more anxious about being in such an unfamiliar situation. Yet, I ran around the city and had a lot of fun, ordered food the best I could in a foreign language, and got a ticket to explore Tokyo Tower. It was a lot of fun casting away my social inhibitions. Reflecting on my time in Japan, I wonder if I do willingly wear the chains of social anxiety for a specific purpose. Despite all the distress associated with my anxiety, it does serve an important purpose to avoid doing anything to be disliked.

When I work with patients, I try to explore both the cause and function of the behavior. Understanding the cause is helpful because it is validating for the patient to contextualize their distress—to make it all make sense and reduce self-blame. Moreover, this approach helps me view the patient in a compassionate and strengths-focused light. Instead of thinking of these behaviors as pathological or nonsensical, we can view them as intelligent behaviors that simply no longer provide us benefits as it did in the past. Anger can be seen as a protective mechanism against vulnerability and dissociation can be viewed as a way to escape from distressing feelings. Even panic attacks could be thought of as a mechanism to protect a person from life-threatening conditions like heart attacks. We can think of avoidance behaviors, like staying at home, as a way to retain control. This could be explained in the context of posttraumatic stress where a person has learned that the world is unsafe. Therefore, from a teleological lens, it makes perfectly reasonable sense that the person may avoid the dangerous outside to protect themselves from being hurt again.

I try to honor these behaviors in therapy. It can be validating to look at a behavior with a slightly more compassionate reframe. These behaviors are not enemies that prevent you from moving toward a life worth living. It's an overprotective friend that used to keep you safe during hard times. This perspective can be helpful to reduce shame and restore a sense of self-efficacy. We can thank the behavior for all of its help and tell them everything is going to be okay. And then you can choose a new behavior that is more consistent with your current goals. Teleology is the exact opposite of determinism; its essence is free will.

As a therapist, teleology and its logical consequences is not an idea that I shove down my patient's throats. Regardless of its validity, I think it is always important to understand the felt experience of the patient. The discussion surrounding teleology without compassion for the patient can be damaging. However, when this idea is brought up appropriately, people can make better sense of their own behaviors. We recognize that all of our behaviors are adaptive in one way, shape, or form, and we can see wisdom within them. We can thank them with genuine appreciation and then choose to take a new path.

17

The Mountain Known as Progress

"What doesn't kill you makes you stronger, stronger."—Kelly Clarkson

Progress is never perfectly linear. Throughout your journey, you will often find yourself zigging up and down the proverbial mountain known as progress. That is why I like to reserve the last couple therapy sessions to normalize these natural ebbs and flows and plan out how to deal with potential lapses and relapses. We can think of lapses like slight setbacks; for example, having a couple poor nights of sleep or the occasional dip in mood. Relapses are often more intense and prolonged. It's kind of like the difference between missing an exit sign and immediately correcting course as opposed to feeling like you are back where you started.

I consider these setbacks to be an important part of the overall therapeutic journey. When patients come into a therapy feeling disheartened about their lapse in progress, I validate their sadness. However, I also tell them that I see this as a good thing. Not because I am a psychopath, but because learning to deal with these setbacks are essential to feeling confident in becoming their own therapist. Through these disappointments you learn that you can shake the boat and rest assured that you can get it back on course. In insomnia therapy, we sometimes talk about the break-it fix-it model. The idea is that we want patients to experiment with intentionally creating some disruptions in their sleep, such as by sleeping in on weekends or spending a little extra time awake in bed, to demonstrate that they can get their sleep back on track. This practice can increase a patient's sense of self-efficacy knowing that the improvements are not a fluke and they can reliably be the person to fix their own sleep.

Of course, dealing with small lapses is much easier than navigating full-blown relapses. It is important to identify yellow flags and plan out how to address them. For example, if your goal is to reduce anxiety in social situations, yellow flags could include avoiding more social situations or being less willing to spontaneously start a conversation. In this case, you might go back to some exposure practice and intentionally plan out of a few conversations you could have with a stranger or call up an acquaintance for lunch. I recall one of my patients who was successfully treated for panic disorder. During a follow-up session, he reported experiencing another panic attack. We used that as an opportunity to explore his resilience in managing that panic attack and how he was able to react with less catastrophic thoughts compared to the beginning of treatment. Instead of worrying that he was going to die, he was able to sit with the sensations and see it for what it was—something very uncomfortable and unpleasant, but ultimately not life-threatening. To reduce his fears of anxiety symptoms, he decided to go back to intentionally practicing some exposures, such as running in place and spinning in his chair, to bring up these unpleasant sensations and sit with them.

Ultimately, I think of working through these lapses and relapses like the process of building muscle. In order to build muscle, you hit the weights and break down the muscles. Afterward, the muscles rebuild themselves bigger and stronger. Similarly, each time you practice the skills, your "therapist" muscle becomes stronger. Pretty soon, you'll be a damn good therapist for yourself.

18

A Clinical Potpourri

Metaphors, Analogies, Experiential Practices and More

"Metaphors have a way of holding the most truth in the least space."—Orson Scott Card

Clinicians love using metaphors and analogies in therapy. There's something remarkable about these playful tongue-in-cheek statements that seem to naturally help people understand an idea better. Perhaps they work by creating new neural pathways and connecting abstract ideas with something that is more familiar. For example, a bodybuilder might find thinking about exposure hierarchies for social situations somewhat abstract until they connect the concept to being like training a muscle. Metaphors and analogies may also increase psychological distance from a situation by allowing us to see a situation from a broader perspective, like watching a storm from afar rather than being right in the eye of the hurricane. There is also just a felt sense of wisdom that comes from these little word nuggets. For example, if you are a caregiver or a people-pleaser, you may logically (but not emotionally) connect with the idea that you need to take care of yourself before you take care of others. However, if someone said that "you have to dig yourself out of prison before you can help someone else" sometimes it just clicks. You resonate with this principle at a level beyond someone just annoyingly telling you to engage in self-care.

One of my clinical supervisors had strong opinions that therapy is not just about providing patients with an education. She thought this approach to therapy to be somewhat paternalistic—a very "do as the teacher says" approach. Unsurprisingly, she did not consider this to be very good therapy. She instead viewed therapy as a collaborative process in which both the patient and the therapist joined together in the co-creation of knowledge. Sure, the therapist had expertise in the treatment of the disorder but the patient also brought expertise in terms of how these principles applied to their life.

A book, however, is not therapy. Communication in a book also happens to be a one-way street. Underlying my supervisor's thought process, I think she understood that simply educating someone would not allow them to develop a truly deep understanding of the concepts. I agree with this point. This is why I encourage folks to practice the skills in this book whenever possible. I want to take you from a surface-level understanding into a deeper experiential understanding of these ideas. At least in cognitive behavioral therapy, we think of the real progress to occur outside the four walls of the therapy room. I hope that this clinical potpourri of fun metaphors, silly analogies, and short practices will be one avenue where I can bring this book to life. I hope they invoke a stronger sense of emotional connection with the ideas, allow you to embrace them in your life, and make you feel just a little wiser afterward.

The Unwanted Guest

Denise was preparing for her annual family party. She had gone through great pains to ensure a picture-perfect event. Personalized party favors, oven-roasted rosemary chicken and potatoes, and various fun planned events for children and adults alike—even the festivities seen in Hallmark movies paled by comparison. Denise wanted nothing more than for her family to delight in her meticulously crafted festivities. She extended an invitation to pretty much all of her family, and everyone was delighted to come. On the day of the party, Denise's eyes poured over all her loved ones: her aunt

Lily, uncle Rob, sister-in-law Sophie, nephews George and Chris, Grandma Edith. Wait ... Grandma Edith? No that couldn't be right, Grandma Edith should have been away for her annual trip to Maui. Denise had intentionally planned the party around Grandma Edith's travels to avoid having her at the party. Grandma Edith was the cantankerous sort that could spoil the merriment like a glass of milk left out on a hot summer's day in Arizona. She was the grim reaper of joy. Last year, Grandma Edith had made several of the nephews and nieces cry because they were being too loud while playing Mario Kart. Denise's stomach was in knots thinking about what sort of nasty comments Grandma Edith would pull out of her bag of evils tonight. As a result of her presence, Denise could not focus on any of the other more pleasant parts of the party. Denise had missed the forest for the unsightly tree.

The Unwanted Guest metaphor is a fun story that embodies the principles of acceptance and commitment therapy. We become fixated on the problems of our life and the other beautiful parts disappear from our field of vision. I suspect we all have a version of Grandma Edith in our life. Maybe our Grandma Edith is a form of chronic pain. Maybe she is an unfortunate work-related situation or an annoying acne scar on your left cheek. Our excessive focus on the Grandma Ediths of our lives can make us forget the rest of the party. If possible, I would invite you to welcome Grandma Edith into your house. We can force her out and lock the doors but I imagine some lasting vestige of her is going to continue to haunt the walls. So welcome her, as well as any other guests that you might not consider to be your favorite person in the world, into your life with a smile on your face and a sense of ease in your heart. And if you're looking for a heartfelt and powerful way to bring this idea alive, there is a wonderful poem called "The Guest House" by Rumi. In the poem, Rumi encourages people to welcome all experiences—pain, sadness, joy, thoughts and feeling—into the home and to be grateful for each visitor because they all impart upon us a valuable lesson.

The Sunset and the Beachball

Elliot was spending a lovely day at the beach. He had spent his time building sandcastles worthy of a king, swimming in the clear waters with the infinite horizon in front of him, and suntanning under a palm tree while enjoying a novel by Haruki Murakami. For the cherry on top of a wonderful day, Elliot was excited about watching the beautiful sunset while wading in the sea, the water lightly caressing his body. He found an ideal place to observe the sunset neatly tucked on the side of the mountain range, away from other people and distractions. It was ideal anyway, until a bright-colored beach ball bumped up against his shoulders. Slightly bemused, Elliot pushed the beach ball out of the way. However, the ball floated right back to Elliot's side like a cat to its favorite windowsill. More frustrated now, Elliot threw the beach ball as far as he could, but to no avail. No matter what Elliot did the ball would always find its way back home—right by his side. In a last ditch attempt, Elliot attempted to drown the beach ball by pushing the ball down under the water. This approach worked for a few moments but then the beach ball slipped through his grasp and the power of buoyancy plopped the sphere back up, smacking Elliot right in the face.

Elliot came to the grim realization that his circular friend was here to stay. So he gave up on the idea of getting rid of the ball and decided that they could watch the sunset together. He turned away from the tiny ball and focused his attention toward the much bigger orange ball of fire in the sky. He was captivated by the majesty of the sun, the shimmering water below that fostered a profound sense of belonging, and the backdrop of ever-changing hues as the sun continued to set. At some point, the beach ball continued on its journey to pester another unsuspecting visitor. But Elliot did not even notice its disappearance. He was too focused on the sunset.

The lesson imparted by the beach ball analogy is similar to the unwanted guest. In this case, Elliot's resistance to the existence of the beach ball only made it stick around longer. What we resist tends to persist. And suppressing things that are unwanted can make them return at twice the force. It also takes our focus away from what truly matters—the sunsets of our own lives. I invite you to practice letting go and turning your focus on your own sunset. Who knows, you might even find that when you stop focusing your attention on the things that bother you, they might just disappear into the horizon.

The Pink Elephant

I would like to invite you into a short practice. For the next minute, I want you to think about anything that you want. Except for a pink elephant. Your mind has infinite possibilities to ponder but you are not allowed to imagine this four-legged land animal with its big floppy ears and long trunk. Go ahead and practice now.

If you went through this exercise, I suspect that the pink elephant made its way back to the center of your mind a few times. Possibly many times. I find that this practice really brings to life the message in the story of Elliot and the beachball. When we try to push away a thought, image, or urge, it tends to make its way back into our mind. Paradoxically, if you were to try and intentionally focus on the image of the pink elephant, you would probably be distracted. I encourage you to see how it would feel to entertain even the most unusual and uncomfortable thoughts. What would it be like to dispassionately observe these thoughts and allow them in your mind rather than pushing them away. Be curious about your experience and reflect on what happens afterward.

The Itchy Body Scan

While I have your mind filled to the brim with pink elephants, I'd also like to invite you to another very short practice. Take a moment to settle into a comfortable position, spine straight and shoulders relaxed. I'd like you to scan your body for an itch. Take your attention to your feet and legs, your left elbow, right shoulder, buttocks, back of your neck, or anywhere else that you'd like to bring into attention.

If I were a betting man, I'd bet you found an itch.

Attention can be a funny thing. When we start to look for something, we usually find it. For example, in insomnia, we are often looking for evidence that we did not rest well at night, such as headaches, heavy eyes, or a general sense of fatigue. In depression, we discount the positives and focus on the negatives. In social anxiety, we are highly attuned to signs of disinterests like frowns or curt replies. The problem is that we use this vague information as evidence that confirms negative beliefs. I must be tired. I am worthless. I am boring.

Instead of using our attention to confirm negative beliefs, I encourage you to really open your senses and be willing to shift your attention to all possible experiences. Maybe my eyes are tired but when I shift my attention to my body, it feels strong. Perhaps I did not do well on the recent botany test but I have been productive in my research and recently presented my work on the impact of climate change on flowering times in black sage at an undergraduate conference. The cute boy seemed disinterested but I really enjoyed reconnecting with an acquaintance at the party. Notice where your attention likes to go and see if you can play around with bringing your attention to a different experience. This practice does not mean you are deluding yourself and shying away from painful moments. It's simply to practice psychological flexibility and demonstrate that we have freedom in focusing on whatever we want. Remember, you'll always find what you are looking for, so make sure you are looking for the right things.

The Passengers on the Bus

Sasha is driving a bus from New York to Albuquerque. Since she was a child, Sasha dreamed of going to Albuquerque and wandering the shopping area in Nob Hill, admiring the Petroglyph National Monument, and experiencing the balloon fiesta. Not to mention,

Bugs Bunny is her favorite Looney Tunes character and he frequently referred to Albuquerque. Sasha felt fortunate to have her bus and wanted to share the goodwill by bringing other folks along the trip. She picks up various passengers: Depression, Anxiety, Shame, among others. The passengers were quiet at first but with time began to heckle her. Anxiety would shout at Sasha that she is driving too fast, but then Shame would tell her that she is driving too slowly. Anger would tell her to change the tunes on the playlist and then Depression would complain about the lack of folk music in her repertoire. Sasha would try her best to accommodate the passengers' numerous and often conflicting needs. Satisfied, the passengers would quiet down for a bit before the complaints would inevitably resume.

One morning, as a chorus of complaints from the passengers rose up about not wanting to go to boring Albuquerque and wanting to head to Los Angeles instead, Sasha finally reached her breaking point. She realized that she was the one in control of the bus and she could drive wherever she pleased! She yelled at the passengers to quiet the heck down and that she was going to Albuquerque whether they liked it or not. They were welcome to stay but she would no longer entertain their complaints. Whenever the passengers tried to get a word in edgewise, Sasha simply let them know that they could leave the bus at any time. After a few more days of driving, Sasha finally arrived at Albuquerque and had a wonderful time. And instead of taking an accidental left at Albuquerque like Bugs Bunny, she went right instead.

Like Sasha, we often have many passengers in our own bus—emotions, judgments, fears, worries—that are constantly voicing their opinions and pulling us in every which way. They often take us away from value-driven behaviors. For example, your goal might be to become an educator by applying for a graduate program in education. However, anxiety might say that you are not prepared and depression will say that you won't be a good teacher. Acquiescing to the passengers might quiet them down for a moment and provide short-term relief, but they will always come back—and their voices become even stronger. I encourage you to be willing to notice what the passengers are saying, but to remember that you are always the driver of your own bus. Follow the deep wisdom inside of yourself and continue driving on to Albuquerque.

The Baseball Game

Steven and James are planning a day out at the golf range. When they arrive, the receptionist informs them that the golf range is fully booked. However, they still had space at the batting cage. James is upset at this unexpected development. He really had his heart set out to play golf. He was first up to bat and the pitching machine began warming up. After missing the first ball, James decided that he hated baseball and did not want to play anymore. He only came out to play golf. In a fit of willfulness, James threw his bat down and sat down in a huff. However, his turn in the cage wasn't over and the pitching machine mercilessly pitched heaters at increasingly higher velocities right at James. Despite James' roaring complaints, the baseballs continued to rain down on the poor man.

Steven was also really looking forward to playing golf. When he was up to bat, he decided that since he couldn't play golf, he might as well try playing baseball. Like James, he had no idea what he was doing, but he was willing to pick up his bat and start swinging. The balls would often zip by him and occasionally he would catch one with his face. However, once in a while, the bat would make an exceptional crack and he would knock the ball out of the park. Regardless of how he ended up in the situation where a pitching machine was shooting fastballs at him at 90 miles per hour, Steven realized there was nothing left to do but to play ball.

I believe that this baseball story is a wonderful example of the difference between willfulness and willingness. I think of willfulness like turning away from life and deciding not to play. On the other hand, willingness is turning toward life and being open, receptive, and engaged in the present moment. Life is often unfair. Sometimes we are placed in situations against our will. In those moments, we can be willful like James and decide to sit with our hands on our bums and let life continually smack us with baseballs. The other option is to be like Steven and be willing to accept what life throws at us and give it our best shot regardless of how stupid we look in the moment. You're there either way so you might as well play some ball.

Alan and the Black Dog

Alan walked around with his black dog named Depression. Depression would try to drag him back every time Alan tried to head out the door. However, the dog would surprisingly offer much less resistance when Alan decided he would rather go to bed. Depression would channel negative thoughts to Alan and made him feel worthless. It chewed up anything that offered enjoyment and meaning in Alan's life. As Alan grew more sad and tired, Depression became bigger and the influence the dog had on Alan became stronger.

Alan began keeping a journal of the things that fed Depression and made him bigger. He also started jotting down the activities that seemed to starve the dog and make Depression a little less imposing. Even though Alan felt that moving through life was like wading through molasses, Alan persevered and went back to taking daily walks at the park and spending time with friends. Alan called his mom at night even though Depression was barking at him to stop and he started going on dates even though Depression sent him negative thoughts about him being a loser. The dog would continue to try and interfere with Alan's life, but Depression's barks became quieter and his teeth didn't have the same vice grip as before. Over time, Alan noticed that he had become stronger and Depression the dog seemed to have shrunk a few sizes. Depression never fully left Alan's side and remained a constant companion, but Alan felt that his relationship with the dog had changed just a little bit.

The story of Alan and his dog can be applied to any psychological disorder: depression, anxiety, insomnia, obsessive compulsive disorder, you name it. In each instance, there will be behaviors that feed the disorder and make it stronger and there will be actions that make the disorder lessen its grip on you. If I have social anxiety then behaviors such as avoiding people and presentations will probably make the phobia stronger. On the other hand, exposing myself to these uncomfortable situations will starve the anxiety and fuel my own strength to handle uncomfortable social situations. These internal struggles may be a constant companion in our lives but we have the ability to choose the behaviors that nourish ourselves and those that starve the beast.

Leaves on a Stream

For this practice, I'd like you to spend a couple minutes visualizing that you are sitting by a stream. I invite you to then observe your thoughts as if they were leaves passing along the stream. If you get carried away by a thought, that's okay. Just imagine bringing yourself back to the bank next to the stream continuing to observe the thoughts. If you wonder whether you are doing this practice correctly, just noticing that this too is simply a thought on the passing stream.

The leaves on a stream practice emphasizes mindfulness with our thoughts. It is a way of attending to thoughts in a non-judgmental way, without attachment to any particular thought. I have had many patients engage in this practice and it is always interesting to get their response. Some folks notice feeling very relaxed whereas others feel that they did not do the practice right. They would tell me that their mind was racing the whole time and they felt very uncomfortable. But there is no right or wrong way of practicing mindfulness. I consider mindfulness a practice of *noticing*—even just the awareness that one is having racing thoughts is mindfulness. The point of mindfulness is not to keep your mind completely still and never have your attention swayed by a thought. The point is simply to observe your experience. The next time you have a thought come up, I encourage you to respond by saying "Oh, I just had a thought" or

"I'm noticing a judgment about myself" and see if you can simply let the thought float away like a leaf on the stream or a cloud in the sky. The act of verbalizing or visualizing the thought helps to create psychological distance from the thought. Understanding that we are not our thoughts frees us from the grip that our brains' random mentations have on our well-being.

The Train at the Station

Tommy is waiting at the train station for a train that will take him to Narnia. He sees a majestic train with a gilded lion at the front of a locomotive and is ecstatic about the prospect of taking this train to his dream destination. While he was waiting for his train to depart, he saw another train that also seemed to be departing for Narnia. It was leaving in five minutes, but this one had the design of the White Witch rather than Aslan the Lion. Tommy decided that he would wait for the first train, so he let the second train pass him by. After a couple hours, Tommy's train still didn't have any updates as to when it would leave the station. A third train heading off to Narnia, however, had made its way onto the station. Tommy considered taking this train since they were both heading off to Narnia. However, the issue was that this train went to Beruna but he wanted to go to the capital Cair Paravel. Tommy decided to let the third train take off without him. And so, trains continued to arrive at the station and depart for Narnia. Each time, Tommy found reasons to let the trains leave without him on it and he continued to wait for the moment that his ideal train would finally depart.

Like Tommy, many of us are also waiting for the right conditions—our own perfect train—to finally depart so we can head toward our desired destination. We wait months, years, perhaps a lifetime, for the stars to align. But what if they never do? Should we wait for the perfect train that may never depart or should we throw ourselves into uncertainty and discomfort by taking a train that is imperfect but would allow us to move toward our goals? If we wait for the perfect time, we may end up watching our lives pass us by and never get anywhere at all. Rather than the train that never leaves the station, perhaps the real perfect train is the one you can take right now, even if it awkwardly bumbles along to your destination. And the perfect moment can only be now because now is the only moment that exists.

The Shovel and the Prison

Clinicians sometimes make the analogy that helping a patient in therapy is like helping someone break out of prison. The therapist cannot be the one to open the door. They don't have the key. The therapist also can't break open the jail from outside because the walls are too tough. The only thing the therapist can do is to give the patient a shovel and tell them to start digging like hell.

For better or worse, research indicates that patient-related factors, such as motivation and engagement in therapy, are strongest predictors of outcomes. The therapist provides validation about the patient's suffering, supports motivation for change, and offers evidence-based shovels to the patient. But only the patient can truly save themselves and dig themselves out of their mental prison. I wish I could relieve every person's suffering but I fully accept my limitations. I am not Obi-Wan Kenobi and I don't have the Jedi mind tricks to make someone suddenly want to change their life. However, if you are considering therapy or are open to the strategies presented in this book, then I think that is a fantastic sign that you stand to benefit from the therapeutic process. And of course, I'm happy to sit with any patient that comes through the door, provide validation and instill hope in therapy, and give them the right shovel to start digging.

19

Words from the Wise

Lessons from Clinical Supervision

"If I have seen further, it is by standing on the shoulder of giants."—Sir Isaac Newton

The pathway toward a career in clinical psychology requires a lot of training. And I mean *a lot*. Four years for the bachelor's degree, two years for the master, another four (or more) to obtain the doctorate, which includes a one-year predoctoral internship, and then a year of supervised practice before finally becoming a licensed psychologist. That's like a bajillion years (I'm not a math major). Consequently, I've had more than my fair share of clinical supervisors over the years and I have received quite a few clinical pearls from these experiences that I can now impart into you. Although I could stretch each one into their own chapters, I don't want to bore you and decided to turn this into a sort of "Top 10 Lessons" chapter. I find that lists make our brains feel happy and it is an easy way to process information. There is also something intrinsically fun about lists which is probably why channels like WatchMojo are so popular. Anyway, here are some lessons from clinical supervisors that I have found useful and I hope they add some value to your life too.

Sometimes the Insight Is Enough

Early in my clinical career, I always thought something more than insight was needed to make a change for the patient. After some exploration, my patients and I would eventually get to the "Aha!" moment. In the front of my mind, I see these eye-opening insights as a good thing that gives the patient a better understanding of their own psychology. In the back of my anxious brain, however, I would wonder about what to do afterward. "So, we have identified that your feelings of incompetence stem from your mom constantly making you feel like you weren't good enough. Now what?" It felt like I adjusted the patient's prescription lens to see their crap more clearly on the floor. But I wasn't sure how to go about cleaning it up.

It was therefore reassuring when my supervisor, Dr. Robertson, said that it can often be immensely useful for the patient to be aware of the triggers for their "trauma response." This insight can be validating for a patient and better positions them to regulate distressing emotions. The patient would then feel more capable to respond effectively when the trauma response is active. For example, one of my patients was very self-critical and she would feel extreme shame any time she felt like she had failed. Through our discussions, we identified that this feeling of shame stemmed from her mom constantly telling her that she was not performing up standards. The focus was always on the room for improvement and her mom paid no mind to her daughter's great work. For this patient, the realization of where these judgments of "I'm not doing enough" and "I'm not a good person" originated was helpful to reduce her shame. It wasn't her voice; it was her mom's. This acknowledgment was enough to find an off-ramp from her shame and feel more comfortable with being less than perfect. For other patients who need a little extra push, I still find it useful to identify when they are walking down the uncomfortable beaten path and provide clinical tools to get them on a preferred path. For example, a patient may realize that they are often passive aggressive during arguments with their partners and would like to work on assertive communication. In this case, the patient would benefit from learning interpersonal effectiveness skills.

Similarly, I would encourage you to become more aware of these unhelpful patterns in your life. Perhaps an aversion to shame makes you withdraw or there is a catastrophic worry that keeps you feeling stuck. Noticing when you are walking on that same trodden earth gives you more space to choose a skillful response. Perhaps you can take a few deep breaths to manage the feelings of shame or set up a behavioral experiment in your mind to evaluate whether your worries are true or not. These strategies will provide an off-ramp to escape the beaten path.

Be Good at a Couple Things

One of my first clinical supervisors, Dr. Milligan, is a specialist in child and adolescent psychology. A simple lesson that she imparted about ways to develop positive self-esteem was to get good at a couple things. Her reasoning was that being proficient in only one area puts you at risk of placing all your eggs in one basket. The problem with being only good at one thing was that if something happens that makes you feel crappy in your specific area of competence, then it would be easy for your ship of self-esteem to capsize into a sea of mediocrity. Let's say you placed all your worth into being a good student. You then receive some harsh feedback on your term paper, or your lazy friend who only studies the night before the exam receives a higher grade than you, these experiences could lead to a shattering blow to your self-confidence.

I ran into a similar issue in my teens. I didn't consider myself particularly great at most things. And being good at catching Pokémon or playing card games weren't exactly strong sources of pride. My academic ability was the only socially acceptable area where I felt somewhat competent. That isn't to say I was exceptional either (my high school was full of overachievers) but I was capable enough to be a rather hot commodity when deciding on members for group projects. Once I graduated from high school, however, I experienced the classic story of university shining a spotlight of mediocrity on a student who thought they were hot stuff back in the high school days. Given that I didn't really have a specific reason for going to university, except for the fact that it was the typical Asian kid's next step, I struggled with a lack of motivation. I didn't know what I wanted to do and at the time I wasn't the industrious sort of person who could do work for no reason. My grades suffered and my picture was next to the encyclopedia definition of average. My less than stellar grades were particularly disheartening because it's not like I was engaging in university life in other ways. Instead, I would spend most of my time meandering aimlessly in the bookstore or engaging in my duties as part of the "go-home" club. I lost the only thing that buoyed my self-esteem and I floated purposelessly, with mild depression and anxiety, for a good portion of my undergraduate studies. It wasn't until the end of second year when I started to adjust to university-level coursework and did better in my classes that my self-esteem began to shift. Building on this momentum, I also joined as a research assistant for a few psychology labs. I started taking leadership roles in these settings, built up a stronger social network with like-minded folks, and was fortunate to have wonderful supervisors who believed in my potential when I couldn't believe in myself. I also started going to the gym and getting into weightlifting (big thanks to my friend Wylie for pulling me into the iron temple).

These days, I'm still terrible at a lot of things. However, I am able to spread my confidence eggs into a few different baskets. I still feel good when I hit the gym. I am happy when I spend time with family and friends. I can also pare down my work into several areas of competence. For example, I feel confident in my ability to support patients as a clinician, conduct research as a scientist, and communicate ideas in my writing and talks as an educator. So even if someone decides to send me a nasty comment about my horrible writing, I can still fall back on the other parts of my life that keeps my self-esteem intact.

I also invite you to cultivate a couple things in your own life to build your own self-esteem. It could be learning a new language, being more active in your life, or developing a new skill. You can also break something you are good at into multiple parts. For example, perhaps your work requires you to be socially competent, a math whiz, and an excellent orator. And if you are trying to build out another area of competence, remember that sucking at something is the first step toward being sort of good at something.

People Can Do Hard Things

I occasionally have the habit of treating my patients as though they were fragile dishes. They tell me that something sounds very hard and my instinct is to start thinking of ways to make it easier. For example, if a patient is resistant toward the idea of talking to a stranger every day as part of exposure practice, I might fold and find another social interaction that is more comfortable. I suspect this automatic reaction results partly from my mild need to be liked and partly from a desire to not cause suffering to the patient—taking the ethical principle of non-maleficence meaning "do no harm" to its extreme. The problem with this approach is that sometimes medicine is bitter. And diluting potentially effective medicine just because it does not taste good is not doing right by the patient.

Shying away from providing patients with helpful tools because I worry about a potentially aversive reaction is a disservice to them. In some ways, it is a selfish action and does not actually take into consideration the human being in front of me. The more patient-centered action would be to trust in the patient's resilience and explore together the right path forward. My supervisor Dr. Posner once said that he would never take an off-ramp for treatment decisions based on anxiety. He was willing to be compassionately flexible in his decision-making but his decisions would never be because of his or his patient's discomfort. In fact, he often dared to go where angels feared to tread. For example, if a patient was worried that other people would laugh at them if they started a conversation, he would probably say: "Okay, let's see if they really would laugh at you. Let's see if you will really die of embarrassment as a result!" I don't think I have it in me to take such an approach, but I think there is an important lesson here—that it is important to model a sense of trust in the patient. Similarly, I believe you, the reader, is also stronger than you might think. You can do the hard stuff. You got this.

Identify the Inner Wish or Need

My first clinical supervisor, Dr. Cheng would often ask me the same question: "What is this patient's inner wish or need?" He was trained under a psychodynamic orientation though the teaching he provided at our clinic was primarily cognitive behavioral. His clinical style was therefore a blend of bridging past experiences with the present moment experience. For example, a patient may have been called dumb often in the past. In an attempt to fulfill their need to feel smart, the patient may spend a lot of time filling the therapy space with their thoughts and opinions.

I believe the importance of identifying the inner need comes from our ability to understand the patient's goals and decide on effective behaviors that can meet the inner need. For example, let's say my wish is for my wife to show love by initiating more in the relationship, such as holding my hand or asking me to go on dates. I would then need to consider whether my behaviors are consistent with getting my needs met. If I am being passive aggressive and silently fuming on the inside about the fact that this need is not being met, these behaviors are probably unlikely to get my wife to be more spontaneously affectionate. However, if I were to express this need and reinforce the behavior by thanking her, the chances of me getting an impromptu kiss becomes more probable. I think this lesson can be distilled into understanding your inner wish and identifying the behaviors that are most likely to have that need met.

The Wisdom Is Inside

A core principle of certain therapies, such as humanistic therapy and dialectical behavior therapy, is an innate trust that each patient already has the wisdom to change. Our goal as therapists is simply helping the patient access their wisdom. This is known as "wise mind" in dialectical behavior therapy. That is also why humanistic therapy simply offers the ingredients believed necessary for the patient to become their authentic self through a genuine relationship formed through empathy and unconditional positive regard.

In dialectical behavior therapy, Dr. Robertson taught me a very elegant principle for understanding how to support folks with borderline personality disorder. At the root of borderline personality disorder there is inherently instability. The goal then is to help work the patient to find their centered wisdom. People with borderline personality disorder tend to feel like they are constantly swinging from one end of the continuum to the other. Therefore, I see my goal to notice where they are in this teeter-totter and put some weight on the other end to help them feel balanced. If a person is experiencing unmanageable emotions, then distress tolerance and emotion regulation is needed to provide some centering. If the person is dissociating, then the therapeutic work should be focused on working with the patient to sit with their feelings. If we assume both ends of the spectrum to have their own unique truths, then finding this balance naturally helps to bring upon a centered wisdom.

One of my patients, Doreen, was always able to access her inner wisdom in therapy. For example, she would be able to express very articulately why it was important to prioritize herself rather than constantly work until she burned out. She had the awareness that some amount of self-care would make her even more efficient at work. It was a win-win. But in the moments at night when she knew she should be in bed ready for sleep, the sense of urgency of needing to get work done made it hard to access the same wisdom she readily shared with me in session. She had the inner wisdom but she could not access it when it was most important.

In this case, I understood that there was no need to be the wise oak tree and impart any wisdom. Instead, the goal was to help her access her own inner wisdom in the moment when her distress clouded the wiser parts of her mind. To help Doreen get out of autopilot, we combined regular mindfulness practice with the STOP skill. The acronym stands for stop, take a step back, observe, and proceed mindfully. During the night, she was literally asked to freeze in moments of urgency, take a physical step back, and take a few breaths. After taking this mindful moment, she could then proceed with the actions most consistent with her values. This strategy forced her to step away from her feelings of urgency, which then allowed her to better respond in the moment.

Stay Grounded in Reality

At the core of obsessive compulsive disorder (OCD) is doubt. People with OCD tend to question reality, like doubting whether a door is locked even after they just checked the locks six times, whether their clothes are really clean even if they just came fresh out of the laundry, or whether their thoughts will lead to someone else getting hurt even if they logically know that this magical connection does not exist. OCD gets us to stray away from reality and we start living in the story that the disorder has created for us.

The common evidence-based treatment for OCD is exposure and response prevention therapy. This treatment works similar to an exposure for an anxiety disorder. You bring up a distressing OCD-related situation (exposure) and then stop yourself from engaging in the compulsion (response prevention). To bring this concept to life, a person with OCD tendencies about contamination may have obsessions about their hands being dirty. Their compulsion would be to wash their hands many times. An exposure and response prevention protocol would get the patient to touch something dirty and then sit with the distress rather than immediately going to wash their hands in the sink. In theory, the brain will learn that there is no harm that will come from not washing the hands and the distress should reduce over time. As Sir Isaac Newton once wisely said: "What goes up, must come down."

Exposure and response prevention therapy continues to be the mainstay treatment for OCD. More recently, however, I was introduced to a novel OCD treatment called inference-based cognitive behavioral therapy. The core idea behind this therapy was that we do not need to engage with the doubt and instead stay grounded in reality. In some ways, exposure and response prevention therapy embraces uncertainty. The practice essentially implies that we don't know what will happen so let's sit with the discomfort and test the worry of whether stepping on a crack will indeed break your mother's back. However, inference-based therapy does not even bother entertaining the OCD-conjured story. The focus of this therapy is increasing certainty by focusing on the five senses. If I worry whether my clothes are clean or not, I look at it. It looks clean. I smell it. It smells clean. Great, I'm not going to engage with the OCD story that the clothes are not clean despite what reality is shouting at me.

I discussed this lesson of staying grounded in reality in the context of OCD, but I think the lesson can apply broadly to life itself. We often create stories in our minds that may or may not be consistent with reality. That other people don't like us. That we won't succeed even if we try. That we are worthless. The problem with trying to solve problems based on stories that our minds have created is that it is ultimately ineffective and unhelpful. Instead, I encourage you to lean into reality regardless of whether the facts of life are beautiful or ugly. Being willing to see what is truly in front of you is the path to freedom.

Don't Just Be Smart, Be Wise

During my postdoctoral fellowship, one of my clinical supervisors made the distinction between being a smart therapist and a wise therapist. She said that a smart therapist is fantastic at getting out of problems. The smart therapist will understand why a patient had a tough time with a specific clinical tool and help them successfully practice the skill the next time. A wise therapist, however, would have never had the problem in the first place. She thought I was a smart therapist but I needed to work on being a wise therapist. Specifically, if I could spot potential pitfalls in the distance and help with workarounds, then I would never have to help the patient climb back out of the hole.

I think this lesson can be useful for people in general. I suspect you are all competent individuals and can handle problems as they crop up in your life. At the same time, I wonder if there is any way we can also become like a wise therapist and avoid possible pitfalls before you need to spend all your efforts pulling yourself back up. Perhaps this means infusing some more mindfulness into your life and learning to respond based on values rather than react solely on emotions. I also think of coping ahead and spending some time thinking about things you can do in the moment that will serve you well in the future.

Validate the Grain of Truth

A common teaching when therapists are starting to learn dialectical behavior therapy is to "validate the valid." The idea is that no matter how black-and-white a person's thoughts are, there is always something within the statement that can be validated. For example, a patient might say "all therapists are terrible" which is a somewhat hurtful, not-fully-valid statement. But a therapist who is compassionate and willing to find the grain of truth could empathize with the patient's poor past experiences in therapy that led to this belief. This ability to validate what is valid helps a patient feel more understood and paradoxically, more willing to let go of their extreme views.

We are often our own worst enemy in many ways. We have a lot of compassion for other people's suffering but don't extend ourselves the same courtesy. The problem is that we can get stuck on the extreme of either end of the polarity and judge ourselves for having the thought. For example, we may say to ourselves "I'm a total loser" and feel an overwhelming sense of shame. However, attempts to try and think the opposite thought generally do not work. People may think therapists will just say "no you are not a loser—you're a winner" which will usually have little impact on the patient's well-being. But that's not what this practice is about; in fact, I encourage you to lean into the initial judgment and validate what is valid. Perhaps you might say "well, I'm not exactly where I want to be in certain areas of my life" and see how it feels to validate yourself without using such an extreme statement. The judge-y version of you may be willing to let go of some of its hatred because you were willing to validate the grain of truth.

Pick the Right Arrow from Your Quiver

My supervisor Dr. Manber authored a book on delivering treatments of chronic insomnia using case formulation, which if you remember essentially can be boiled down to the fifty-dollar question: "What is maintaining this person's problem?" Unsurprisingly, Dr. Manber would always ask me to think critically about what clinical tool might be helpful for the patient. The analogy she liked to use was that we as therapists have a quiver full of arrows and we needed to carefully pull out the right arrow for different situations. To put this principle into practice, let's say a patient is struggling with difficulty falling asleep. Further exploration identified that the person finds it hard to quiet his mind at night because his ruminative thoughts tend to creep in when he is alone at night. In this case, the right arrow was to help the patient find ways to be the director of his own mind rather than let his thoughts take him to dark places. At the beginning of each night, the patient decided that he would start thinking about going on a fantasy adventure and imagine himself travelling to different regions of the world. With this practice, he found this pre-sleep period to be more enjoyable and slept more soundly.

Throughout this book, you've collected a number of different arrows to flexibly incorporate in your life. I encourage you to become your own therapist by choosing the right arrow as different challenges present in your life. For example, if you are noticing a slight dip in your mood, then it may be worthwhile to incorporate some behavioral activation, or if you notice that a fear of uncertainty has gripped you, then taking a curious stance and engaging in a few behavioral experiments could be rather useful. In therapy, I like to say to patients that we are both experts. I am the expert on treatments of mental health and the patient is the expert of themselves. Now, you have become the expert of both: You were always the expert of yourself and you now have all the know-how of a burgeoning therapist. I encourage you to trust in your own wisdom and pull out the specific arrow that will vanquish the monster.

Therapy Is About Giving Patients a Choice

The mindfulness principle of taking a non-judgmental approach is one that resonates a lot with me—perhaps to a fault. My desire to not ascribe judgments may be one reason why I don't usually have a strong emotional response to what people tell me in therapy. If someone told me they were recently served divorce papers, I wouldn't necessarily think that is inherently a good or bad thing. Of course, I would be curious to ask about their experience and share a lot of compassion if the end of their marriage was something that caused them great suffering (or celebrate with them if this was something that was a source of joy). Similarly, I don't have specific expectations about what it means for a patient to succeed in psychotherapy. Whether they decide to change or remain the same, I am their biggest supporter because I don't think there is one right way to live life.

I remember my supervisor Dr. Carney once say to us in a clinical supervision meeting, "Therapy is not about making a change, it's about giving patients a choice." I love that idea and I think there is a lot of truth in the statement. My belief is that distress comes as a function of a lack of perceived freedom. In the context of sleep for example, there is a difference between someone who can easily fall asleep but decides to play video games until late at night and the person who really wants to fall asleep but cannot. The lack of perceived control of sleep processes creates significantly more distress for the second person.

I come to therapy from a place of curiosity. I don't know what is right for you so let's figure it out together. Then let's work toward your goals. I also like to play devil's advocate when my patient starts discussing their goals. Why is this important to you? Why not continue with your current pattern of behaviors? Is this goal coming from your own desire or somebody else's expectations? This practice offers a refreshing conversation with the patient and helps me understand their goals in relation to their values.

I also believe that we all need to recognize that actions have consequences. As adults, we make big boy choices and accept big boy consequences. For example, some of my patients want excellent sleep and they are willing to wake up at the same time every day as a means toward this goal. For other patients they are willing to accept slightly less optimal sleep in order to snuggle with their partner in the mornings and sleep in on weekends. Both are okay and I encourage you to make your choice with conviction. Regardless of which path you decide to pursue, I am genuinely happy for you as long as it feels consistent with your values.

20

Growing Your Garden of Happiness

"There is no path to happiness. Happiness is the path."—
Gautama Buddha

One of the things that I really appreciated about my parents is that they were more interested in my interests rather than pushing me toward their own version of success and excellence. They didn't pressure me to get straight As in school or push me to be a doctor or an engineer. If I was happy, then that was enough. It was quite a departure from the typical tiger parents that characterize East Asian families. I am very grateful to have my mom and dad.

I therefore saw happiness as an important and noble pursuit. The tricky part of happiness, however, is that it can be a somewhat elusive feeling. Sometimes we are in a situation that we know logically should make us happy—perhaps our relationships are flourishing, things are going well at work, there is time and freedom to pursue our values, but we are still feeling low. We may even judge ourselves for our lack of appreciation for everything that is going well in our life and then feel even worse. In contrast, there are times when happiness stops to visit us even when our lives are full of strife, like a butterfly gently landing on our finger underneath a tumultuous storm.

It perhaps goes without saying that chasing happiness usually leads to happiness being nowhere to be found. To build on the analogy of happiness as a butterfly, when we try to pursue the butterfly, the little critter will likely fly away. If we were to somehow manage to grasp it in our hands, it would surely die. Thus, the pursuit of happiness can be damaging to the goal of being happy. The question then is how we can attract these butterflies into our life. Instead of chasing butterflies, my encouragement would be to work on building a garden filled with lush greenery that provides a home for the butterflies to reside. When they visit your garden, you can take a moment to admire the butterflies during their brief sojourn in your garden. It's a mindful endeavor because you are not attached to their presence because your focus is on cultivating your garden. But for that moment you can be fully immersed in your appreciation. Even if there is a time where no butterflies visit, you pay it no mind. After all, you are focused on tending to your garden.

Thinking of happiness as butterflies in a garden is a pleasant analogy, but the question is what does it mean to tend to your garden? I can't speak to your own personal garden but I can tell you how I tend to my garden. I think my garden flourishes when I am living a values-consistent life. For me, this means focusing on my relationships and calling my mom in the evening or having a meaningful conversation with my friends. It means prioritizing health and hitting an upper body session at the gym or taking time for my hobbies like learning a nocturne by Mozart on the piano. Tending to my garden also means growing as a therapist, a scientist, and as a writer. It's wonderful when I am able to provide values to patients and readers, and the occasional kind words I receive from these folks is something I cherish wholeheartedly. Finally, I see tending to the garden as being in the moment. As I am writing this section of this book, I am enjoying a nice double espresso in a hotel in Shanghai while visiting my wife's family. All these experiences cultivate my garden and make it more likely for the butterflies of happiness to decide to spend some time in my garden.

Similar to the Values chapter, I encourage you to consider what are the behaviors that would help cultivate your own garden. Perhaps you feel the best when spending time with certain people in your life or when you are studying a new language. The flowers in your garden may be in full bloom when you are actively participating in life and refining your craft to provide value to other people. Tending to your garden could also be as simple as mindfully enjoying a cup of coffee in the morning and basking in the sunlight.

Even when we do all the right things, we may not always be happy. But we can rest content knowing that we are living in a way that gives us the best chance for happiness.

21

Coloring the Tapestry of Our Lives

"The meaning of life is just to be alive. It is so plain and so obvious and so simple. And yet, everybody rushes around in a great panic as if it were necessary to achieve something beyond themselves."—Alan Watts

It would not truly be a book on therapy without at least making an attempt, however feeble and potentially fruitless, to discuss the meaning of life. Perhaps the greatest protection from existential nihilism, at least in the way that some folks inappropriately use nihilism as a reason to do absolutely nothing with their lives, is to find one's reason for living. Together, I hope we can work to try and fill the tapestry of our lives with colors that suffuse our life with meaning.

Over the course of this book, there are perhaps a few different approaches to start finding meaning in our lives. First and foremost, I believe a significant amount of meaning comes from an intentional focus on our values and working toward the whys of our lives. If we are taking a journey toward our values, then there is meaning infused in every step that we take toward these distant North Stars. I know this has been oft-repeated in the book, but my first encouragement is to take some time to really consider what are the values of your life. Whether these values are related to family, adventure, creativity, altruism, playing, or something else, figure out the whys of your life and take a few steps toward those values.

Some folks may consider this journey pointless if the destination always ends in death. In the spirit of the title of this book, I think a little reframing of death can be helpful. Irvin Yalom's ideas can be helpful in thinking about death not as something that renders everything meaningless; rather, the concept of death allows life to truly flourish. If life were to truly go on forever, there would be little reason to do much of anything. Instead, it is the finiteness of life that drives us to make meaning out of our temporary existence. The Stoic philosopher Epictetus once said that existence is actually rather long; it is simply that we are truly living for a fraction of this time. There is much opportunity for life to happen if we are present, intentional, and willing to accept all experiences.

Another practice that can be used to infuse meaning into our lives is to leverage our own psychological flexibility. Like a telescope, we humans have a unique power to change the focus of our lens and how we perceive the world. For example, if we were to tune our perspective on a universal scale, everything may appear meaningless. In a couple hundred years, nobody will remember us, and the universe will eventually experience its own end following the heat death of the universe. If we compressed Earth's 4.5 billion year history into a 24-hour clock, humans would have only existed for a few seconds. Our individual lives are even more fleeting. So what's the point anyway?

We can certainly use this information to maintain a crushing sense of depression and a lack of willingness to do anything. However, a change in our interpretation of the same facts can lead to a different experience. If you apply the same ideas to work up the courage to apply to your dream job or ask out your crush, then this "universal perspective" could be quite functional. After all, everything is meaningless so we might as well go for what we want. We can also use our psychological flexibility to narrow our focus. Even if there is no significance to be found under a time horizon of a billion years, there is meaning in the here-and-now. It may not matter to the universe if we go help out our grandma with baking cookies or make time to call our mom, but it certainly matters to them. Grandma will cherish the time spent with you and your mom will be happy to know that her child is doing well. In the present moment, the small actions matter. Whether it is holding a door for someone, sending an old friend a message that you are thinking of them, or making a small donation to a young child in Ghana to provide her with school supplies, it matters. It's important to remember that each person's lens is different. It may not matter to you, but it could matter to someone else. I invite you to be willing to refocus your lens on occasion just to see whether the world looks different from a new perspective.

Some folks unwittingly use this perspective-taking to invalidate themselves. I had a patient who struggled with grief associated with an ectopic pregnancy, but did not allow herself to process these emotions. Her reasoning was that other people had it worse than her. She was generally healthy, had a supportive relationship, and came from a strong educational background. It felt wrong of her to bemoan her stroke of poor fortune. In this case, she used her psychological flexibility in a way that made it hard to validate her own suffering and to properly grieve for her loss. The analogy I used to soften her own views toward her suffering was that regardless of whether someone is six or sixty feet under water, they are both drowning. And that it is okay to acknowledge one's own pain even if other people are also dealing with life's hardship.

The use of this perspective shift can also be helpful to manage suffering. When we are enjoying the moment, it might be nice to zoom into the moment and really live in the here-and-now without thinking too much about the future or worrying about the past. On the other hand, it can be helpful to assume a broader perspective if we feel like our life is in the toilet. We can zoom out and take a mountain's view of our life. Yes, it's hard right now, but you can look down with the wisdom that the hero's journey would not make for much of an interesting story without adversity.

This concept of separating ourselves from the moment is similar to the one of "decentering" in acceptance and commitment therapy. We often feel fused with our thoughts and emotions. Decentering is a way for us to create space between us and the experience. It's like the difference between having a book be very close to you so you can only see a few blurry words and moving it further away so you can see the whole page. Mindfulness practices of learning to observe our thoughts, physical sensations, and emotions can be helpful to create a sense of psychological distance.

A lovely idea that I find helpful in making a lot of meaning out of our actions comes from reading Irvin Yalom's works and his concept of the rippling effect. That is, a small act is akin to dropping a small stone in the middle of a lake. The initial impact is small and unassuming; the visible ripples created from the stone hitting the water lasts but a brief moment before it disappears to the naked eye. However, the beautiful part of this phenomenon is that the ripples continue to echo throughout time and space in a way that we simply cannot see in the moment. Similarly, the small things that I have done may continue to reverberate and significantly impact another person's life. I remember my graduate school supervisor was away for a couple weeks at a research conference and they asked me to take the lead on a guest lecture for their undergraduate course in psychopathology. I agreed to the proposal and conducted a short lecture on treatments of chronic insomnia. A couple years later, one of the research assistants in my lab was accepted into a clinical psychology graduate program. I sent her an email congratulating her on her achievement, and she sent a reply noting that it was the lecture I gave on insomnia that motivated her to join the lab and ignited her passion for sleep research. She is currently studying pediatrics sleep and will go on to do a lot of amazing things in the field, creating her own ripples into the world.

During my residency year, one of the other psychology residents who specialized in child-focused psychology likened the impact of psychological interventions on children to nudging a plane a couple degrees off course. The initial change in angle may be small, but throughout a person's entire life, the whole of their developmental trajectory may be vastly different by the end of the journey. I invite you to make a positive impact, however small, in another person's life. You never know how much you can change a person's life for the better.

And while I discuss these ideas, I suspect some of you might shrewdly refute this idea by noting the opposite: "Well, you never know how you'll impact another person! It's better to not do anything instead." And those folks would be right to an extent. We can never know how our actions will affect somebody else, but we can always do our best to do good. I think that's enough. There are those of you who will use this reframing as a way to keep yourself stuck, and I suspect many of you who are smart enough to argue the exception, understand very well the rules. So stop using your astute critical thinking powers to maintain the status quo and to keep yourself stuck!

For those of you who feel insignificant in their lives—perhaps they feel like the side character in other people's tales—I'll tell you a story. I remember taking a course in psychology and my professor at the time was talking about the application process for clinical psychology graduate programs. I was thinking about graduate school at the time and was justifiably a little nervous about the acceptance rates, which were fairly abysmal with five to seven percent of applications being successful. Over the recent years, they have precipitously dropped even lower to one or two percent per program. As my professor was going through the application requirements and statistics, there was something he said that was oddly comforting: "Somebody has to get in, so it might as well be you." Of course, he didn't mean *me* specifically. But I found a lot of solace in the comment. Sure, maybe not everybody will get into their desired program, work their dream job, or become rich and successful. But any *one* person can do it. It could be you or me. And why not? Life is often unfair but perhaps sometimes it is unfair in our favor. And I believe the power of taking this perspective is that it gives us the willingness to give it a shot. If we take enough shots, at some point we'll hit that homerun. If broken clocks can be right twice a day, then maybe even regular folks like us can do some amazing things if we just keep on ticking.

Since it's the end of this chapter, I suppose I should muse briefly about death. Obviously, I don't know what happens after death. It's a little arrogant of me to even feel the need to acknowledge my ignorance rather than have it tacitly assumed. I'm sure there are a number of religions and philosophies that will offer much more wisdom. Personally, I like the idea presented by Alan Watts that offers an elegant theory of death: "You are the universe experiencing itself." I like to think after I die, I return to the Universe and I say to the Universe, "Hi, here's what I saw." The Universe listens to my story intently, and after I have finished, pats me on the head and says, "That's wonderful. Thank you for sharing." Here, the meaning of life was simply to live. And there's no right or wrong way to experience life. After all, all of it was life to begin with. Whether I am delighting in joy, falling into despair, healthy as a horse, sick as a dog, spending time with loved ones, or sitting in the dark corner of my room writing this book, all of it falls under the giant umbrella of life. So I encourage you to just live!

And of course, this is just one random guy's opinion.

22

Going from Zero to One

"The journey of a thousand miles begins with one step."—
Lao Zhu

Beyond offering a light and enjoyable read, I genuinely hope that this book helps you make a positive change—however small—in your life. A tiny ripple that continues to echo throughout your life and the lives that you will touch, and so on and so forth. Learning occurs when behaviors change in response to the same stimulus. That is, there is something you are doing differently after reading this book that is more aligned with your goals and values. I also like to read the occasional self-help book and I have noticed that there are many works out there that *feel* helpful in the moment but don't actually lead to any changes in our behaviors. For example, there are some writings that feel like therapy wrapped in a book. Every word seems suffused with wisdom and you can't help but highlight every other sentence. But if we were to put on our pessimistic hats for a moment, the benefits that this mental massage had on our brains probably didn't translate to many changes in the real world. It felt damn good reading it, but we went back to sitting on our bums and scrolling on social media afterward. I would be extremely happy if this were a book that sprung you into action. To begin inching you closer toward your goals. To take a step in becoming your ideal self. And to go from zero to one.

I have dedicated this whole (brief) chapter to see if I can get you to take that first step. The folks who have already started using some of the clinical tools or applying the ideas in this book, wonderful! I encourage you to continue with your great work. And those of you who just wanted a light read and didn't sign up for the author to make annoying meta-comments about needing to get up and start applying the principles of this book into the real-world, this is also a very reasonable response. Still, I think there is some utility in me getting on my soapbox and advocating for change, even if that is at the expense of you finding me a little annoying. I've been working on learning to sit with uncomfortable emotions so this is a great exposure practice for me too.

Fortunately, we don't have to reinvent the wheel to take the first step. Many of the therapeutic strategies and principles that we have already discussed in this book can be leveraged to take the first step. In the spirit of a weird meta-chapter, I'll also enlist some clinicians to support this process. First, the humanistic psychotherapist comes in to help explore your values. She will get you to list a couple things that are important to you. Anything is okay. This is a completely non-judgmental space filled with unconditional positive regard. So feel free to pick something that really resonates with the core of your being.

Next, the behavioral therapist joins the fray to collaborate on developing some specific and actionable goals based on those values. She would help you get more specific about what it would look like if you were moving toward those values. For example, if your values are related to health, then one goal could be doing a five-minute yoga practice or taking a run in the morning. The behavioral therapist will also play all her cards to try and set you up for success. She may apply principles of operant conditioning and get you to reward yourself with a cup of coffee or some time to play a video game after the run. She may also problem-solve possible barriers by getting you to place your running shoes next to your bed so it increases the chances of you going for the run. Another common example of encouraging goal-oriented behavior is putting the TV remote into a faraway cabinet and placing a book next to you instead. For people who aren't very beholden to themselves, but hate the idea of letting someone else down, the therapist might get you to plan a gym outing with a friend so you feel accountable. The lesson: Make goal-oriented behaviors as easy to do as possible and the ones that move you further away from your goal as hard as possible. With the right systems in place, you don't need any of the unreliable stuff like motivation.

The behavioral therapist also recognizes that starting is the hardest part. She encourages you to take a step toward your goals right now. You heard it correctly. Do something consistent with your goals at this very moment. You can do ten jumping jacks, grab a glass of water, or nourish yourself by staring out the window for a mindful moment. Whatever it is, however small, just take that first step. That's all she asks.

Afterward, the cognitive therapist steps in to address any potential unhelpful beliefs or attitudes that get in the way of your goals. For example, some folks may hold beliefs like "it's too late," "I won't feel any better," or "it's too scary." The cognitive therapist may work with the patient to explore the validity and usefulness of the thought. He may encourage you to treat the thought like an experiment and test whether the actions really won't make any difference in your life. Perhaps the small activity you did earlier was already a nice little experiment to see if your mood shifted a little bit. Alongside the cognitive therapist, the clinician who specializes in acceptance-based therapies chimes in and asks you to recall the values of your life. He tells you that your thoughts and emotions are separate from you. And that even if you are scared, that doesn't mean you can't do it scared. This clinician gives you space to process the feelings of grief and shame about not starting earlier. Take a moment to lean into those feelings and allow them to exist. Notice the physical sensations associated with the experience, exploring them with compassion and curiosity, and breath into them. The psychodynamic therapist then comes in, stroking his Freudian-like beard, with an empathetic look. He reflects that the desire to avoid change protects you from feeling vulnerable and potentially being hurt as it might have in the past. At the same time, he understands that you are no longer the same young child. The you right now is stronger. The you right now is smarter. The you right now can become untethered from the past and change your present to forge your own future.

I consider the ultimate goal of psychotherapy is to allow the patient to become their own therapist. Consequently, I encourage you to reflect on your own "formulation"—what are the factors that keep you from moving toward your own life worth living and feeling stuck in the moment? We all have unique locked doors that require a specific key to open. The strategies presented in this book offer different keys for you to try in an attempt to find the one that fits you. The beauty of therapy is that there is never a one-size-fits-all approach, and there may only need to be one or two strategies that are needed to support your well-being. Take a look at your newfound clinical tools and find the one that resonates most with you.

It is completely okay if you are still feeling uncertain or a little overwhelmed. There's no need to leap ahead a thousand miles—just one step is perfect. And if you can't believe in yourself to make this step, I'll believe in you twice as much to make up for your share. You got this, my friend.

23

Eenie-Meenie-Miney-Mo

Choosing Your Therapy

"Everyone has won and all must have prizes."—Dodo in *Alice in Wonderland*

In Lewis Carroll's' *Alice in Wonderland*, various characters were taking a swim in Alice's pool. After the swim, the Dodo bird proposed an unusual challenge which he called the caucus race. The participants were tasked to run around as a way to dry themselves. The rule was that there were no rules. The animals could run around in any way that they wanted, for however long they wanted, until they were dry. And when it came time for the Dodo to decide who had won the caucus race, he issued his famous phrase: "Everyone has won and all must have prizes."

In psychotherapy, there is a phenomenon called the "dodo bird verdict." This phrase was coined by American psychologist, Saul Rosenzweig in 1936 because all empirically-based treatments, i.e., therapies that have been scientifically studied, more or less worked about the same. In the past several decades, there have been various meta-analyses, which are huge analyses that combine the findings from all studies that investigate a similar question, to see which therapy comes up on top. The results agreed with Rosenzweig. Most findings were generally non-significant insofar that all therapies had a similar benefit in improving patient outcomes. Put simply, all therapies have won and all should receive prizes.

The conclusion from this verdict was that the unique ingredients that made each therapy distinct was less important than the common factors that exist in all therapies, such as a positive therapeutic relationship between the patient and therapist and instilling a sense of hope that the therapy will work for the patient. More recent research does suggest that some therapies may be more helpful in certain disorders. This may be the result of a better fit between the active ingredients proposed to make the therapy work and the factors that maintain the disorders. For example, the use of in vivo (real-world) exposures for anxiety disorders are more effective than imaginal exposures. This makes good sense on paper. Having patients with a dog phobia spend time with real dogs instead of just imagining them is likely to be more effective in getting the brain to feel more at ease around the perceived threat. There is also something to be said about treatments that really get into the core of disorders. A couple examples include the use of behavioral experiments to inoculate against the "allergic reaction" to uncertainty in generalized anxiety disorder and cognitive behavioral therapy for insomnia which leverages our understanding of sleep science to improve sleep in folks with chronic insomnia. Many of the evidence-informed strategies remain fairly comparable in their efficacy. Therefore, you can really choose a therapist and therapy that resonates most with your own beliefs and preferences. In this book, we have discussed various therapies and their principles. We've spent time with humanistic therapy and felt the love of its unconditional positive regard; traversed to the past and learned of its grip in our present in psychodynamic therapy; changed the way that we think and how we behave in different situations using cognitive behavioral therapy; and beheld the power and paradox of radical acceptance to life's suffering in third wave therapies. Most clinicians are also eclectic in their therapeutic approach, so you may get a bit of a mishmash of therapies regardless of who you meet in the therapy room. After all, you'd be hard pressed to find a cognitive behavioral therapist who didn't at least try to bring in some amount of genuineness and positive regard to you as a human.

We have established that most therapies work to some degree of efficacy. Therefore, perhaps the therapy you choose is of less importance than the other factors that may be the primary drivers of change. For those who are interested in pursuing therapy, there are certain parts of the therapeutic process that I think are particularly important to reap positive benefits. The first is your own motivation for change. The famous idiom of leading a horse to water but not being able to make them drink comes to mind. I also recently heard of a less common idiom that has a similar meaning: "More than the calf wants to suck, the cow wants to suckle." In either case, the therapist is offering more help than the patient is willing to accept into their lives. Interestingly, research suggests that the most important variables that determine treatment outcome are these patient-related variables of motivation and willingness to change.

The fact that change seems to come from within this does not mean that therapy is useless if you are feeling a little ambivalent. The therapist can absolutely help to support you in deciding on whether this is the right time to seek therapy and if the efforts to make a change are worth the squeeze. You do not need to come into therapy thinking that therapy will definitely be helpful. In fact, an argument can be made that patients who come in with a healthy degree of skepticism may see the best outcomes. If you are dealing with enough crap in your life that warranted a decision to start therapy, it makes perfect sense that you will wonder if therapy can do something for you. The people that seem to benefit most simply come to treatment open and curious about what they will learn. They have justifiable reservations, but they are willing to traverse into the unknown with their therapist.

In his mindfulness-based stress reduction programs, Dr. Jon Kabat-Zinn found that neither people who came into the program thinking mindfulness would solve all their problems nor people who pooh-poohed mindfulness benefited very much. The reason is because when people think of mindfulness as a panacea, they will be sorely disappointed when their unpleasant sensations and experiences continue to persist. And of course, the people who don't believe in mindfulness will probably not truly be willing to accept the potential wisdom that comes with the practice. So come into therapy with an open mind. Be willing to try out the strategies even if there is doubt in the back of your mind. We can be like curious scientists together and evaluate whether the experiment known as therapy has a benefit in your life. If nothing else, it's more fun that way.

Outside of patient-specific factors, there is also significant research to indicate that common therapy factors are important in treatment outcomes. When I say common factors, I mean the parts of therapy that exist in virtually every type of treatment. These common factors include the therapeutic alliance, expectations of therapy, and "specific ingredients." The therapeutic alliance is a specific type of collaborative relationship created by the therapist and the patient which permits fertile grounds for good therapy to unfold. There are various aspects that foster a positive therapeutic alliance: A feeling that the therapist understands the patient and their problem well, a sense that the therapist truly cares about them and likes them as a human being, and trust that the therapist is competent to treat their problem. Perhaps beyond words, it is also important to have a felt sense of connection with the therapist. There's the saying: "You can be the ripest, juiciest peach in the world, and there's still going to be somebody who hates peaches." Therapists are also like peaches. They differ in their personality style, demographics, and therapeutic approach. Some therapists bring into the room their fully authentic and effusive style and show a lot of emotions. Other therapists, like me, take more of a compassionate professional approach. Some patients like me. Others like me a little less. And that's okay. Most therapists will offer a free consultation so you can take some time to figure out which therapist feels like a good fit for you. It's kind of like Tinder for therapy. However, just like dating apps, I encourage you not to get caught up in finding the *perfect* therapist. That sort of therapist probably does not exist and will only lead to disappointment down the road just like if you expect your romantic partner to be without flaws. Instead, find someone who you generally like as a therapist and work toward developing a positive therapeutic relationship. Remember, a healthy and productive relationship goes both ways.

Besides a positive therapeutic relationship, another common

factor is *expectation*, which refers to how much the patient believes the therapy will actually treat their problem. Therefore, it is important for clinicians to foster hope at the outset of treatment by discussing how the therapy works, what the therapy entails, the research supporting the therapy, and why the therapy will work specifically for the patient. A patient will feel more confident about the therapy if the therapist can really showcase to the patient that they understand their problem and can relate the treatment with the patient's problem. For example, a cognitive behavioral therapist may conceptualize a patient's fear of social situations in the context of avoidance and discuss how avoiding social situations relieves anxiety in the short-term but maintains it in the long-term. The introduction of exposures to social situations in a gradual manner to stop feeding into anxious beliefs and start getting a patient to feel more confident in social situations will then make very good sense. The final common factor is that there needs to be some sort of active "ingredient." From a common-factors perspective, the ingredient does not really matter all that much. It could be changing thoughts and behaviors like in cognitive behavioral therapy, warm empathy statements in humanistic therapy, or cultivating non-judgmental awareness in mindfulness-based interventions.

Beyond these common factors, there has been research studying processes in therapy; that is, the things that happen in the therapy room that leads to improved outcomes. Research suggests that therapist self-disclosure and *immediacy*—having conversations about the relationship and dynamics unfolding in the session—were associated with significant positive outcomes. One of my first times applying the use of immediacy was with an early patient of mine who was working on managing their anger. During one therapy session, I noticed that the patient was starting to get a little snappy with me. As a natural people-pleaser, I tend to be quite sensitive to other people's negative emotions, especially when those emotions are directed at me. As a way of bringing immediacy into the therapy session, I reflected on this experience with her: "I'm noticing that you seem upset with me, is that right? Can you tell me what your experience is at this moment?" This question allowed for a very productive conversation to unfold about how she tends to get angry when she thinks other people misunderstand her experience. We were able to then tie this experience to other situations in her life where she felt misunderstood.

More recently, I had a patient with insomnia express that they had thought about dropping out of treatment early in the first session of treatment. She felt that I was being too dismissive of her suffering following a poor night's rest. Although she knew I had good intentions, she felt that her painful experiences were being invalidated by my focus on her being able to function reasonably well despite her chronic insomnia. In response, I apologized and thanked her for her vulnerable disclosure. I encouraged her to let me know any time in the future when it felt like I was being insensitive to her pain. Just like me, this patient acknowledged that she was a bit of a people-pleaser so I wanted to reinforce her willingness to tell me if something about therapy was not going right. I wanted to strike the right balance between reinforcing her compassion toward other people's feelings while simultaneously being willing to be an advocate for herself.

I can almost guarantee that the relational dynamics that occur in the therapy room most certainly also play out elsewhere. Therapy is like a microcosm of real-world interactions so it can be extremely powerful to have these "in-the-moment" conversations. I would encourage both the patient and the therapist to be able to say something like: "I'm noticing this thing that is happening in the room. I'm wondering if you notice it too." This can lead to fruitful conversations about how the patient thinks and also how other people react to the patient's style of interaction. For example, a patient who feels that they don't get much care from loved ones may not realize that they tend to always minimize their own problems. The therapist can reflect to the patient that their unwillingness to share these problems makes them feel less effective and unable to help. The therapist can also venture a guess that other people in the patient's life may feel similarly and that is why they tread lightly to help someone who seems so apparently competent.

I'm a fairly strong believer in equifinality—that many paths can lead to Rome, or in this case, to improved well-being. I do, however, believe it is also important as a scientist-practitioner to encourage you to seek treatments that have scientific support. For example, it may not be appropriate to just receive supportive counselling if you are struggling with a specific disorder. I know that the dodo bird verdict suggests that most therapies can work, but a theoretically sound therapy with a scientific component is essential. For example, you will want to get a sense of the types of therapies out there and whether there is research supporting this therapy for the specific disorder. As well, I invite you to ask the question of whether the therapy seems to make reasonable sense on paper. For example, it makes good sense that exposure therapies work well to reduce anxiety through new learning experiences, e.g., that the airplane will not crash if you ride one. I recognize that the scientific method is not perfect and that treatments without scientific support do not mean that they are bad. However, let's not allow perfection to get in the way of good. I encourage those of you that are deciding to go to therapy to ask the therapist what type of therapy they provide and how the skills learned can specifically target your concerns.

I also realize that it is rather privileged for me to just say "go to therapy." Therapy can be quite expensive and inaccessible. There are services that are low-cost or operate on a sliding scale, with fee reductions depending on your financial background. For folks who have universal healthcare, like in Canada, you can obtain free services, though the wait times tends to be frankly annoyingly long. Some of the low-cost options should be properly vetted and you will want to make sure that the therapist is one that feels like a good fit in terms of personality and training. For those of you who are ambivalent about the utility of therapy, it may be nice to treat the experience as a behavioral experiment. And some people benefit just fine with bibliotherapy and reading a few books that teaches them skills learned in therapy. Of course, I do hope that this book was a little bit helpful to this end.

24

Making Meaning Out of Saying Goodbye

"But I'm sure we'll run into each other again if we continue traveling. Tearful goodbyes aren't our style. After all, it would be embarrassing when we met again."—Himmel the Hero in *Frieren: Beyond Journey's End*

I remember a patient in his mid-thirties who was very passionate about Eastern philosophies. He would often share these principles with me in therapy. He was recounting his experience with the end of a recent romantic relationship. He had loved this person, but through less-than-fortunate circumstances, they did not stay together. Understandably, the experience devastated him. However, he had an incredibly thoughtful way of relating to the painful emotions. Specifically, he understood the importance of these painful experiences as a necessary part of life that exists alongside the more pleasurable sensations. Painful and pleasurable experiences exist in harmony and they imply each other. He understood the impermanence of these experiences and he accepted that the dance of life would continue to change its melodies. Right now, he was going through a sentimental ballad but perhaps soon it would change again to a romantic nocturne. He was willing to accept all these experiences. And he was able to even smile because the pain was direct evidence of how much that relationship meant to him. In the wise words of Winnie the Pooh: "How lucky I am to have something that makes saying goodbye so hard."

The act of saying goodbye *is* hard. Unfortunately, farewells are a shared experience for the social creature known as humans. There were friendships that I thought would last a lifetime only for them to end a fair bit before then. For example, one of my good friends decided to leave our high school friendship group, which had been in existence for more than a decade. He realized that he had outgrown the group and found himself feeling a greater sense of belonging with a new friend circle. He was always a bit of a joker, and we're all a little emotionally constipated, so when I brought up my sadness about his departure, he simply quoted Dr. Seuss: "Don't cry because it's over, smile because it happened." I suspect that he was just being facetious, but there was quite a bit of wisdom that came from his perspective. Though I think his Buddha-esque understanding of the beauty of impermanence was a little beyond me at the time.

The ending of that specific friend group dynamic was painful. But time heals all wounds, I suppose. And I guess Dr. Seuss was right. I'm able to reflect with contented nostalgia at the stupid fun we had over the years. I'm glad that my friend found a group of folks that made him feel like he belonged.

The reason I share this somewhat mundane story is because goodbyes are a natural part of human connections. And therapy is nothing else if not a human connection. The end of therapy can be hard for both the therapist and the patient. The patient may see the therapist as a source of support. One of my patients kindly said that I was like a lighthouse on the shore that she could use as an anchor point whenever she felt lost at sea. For other patients, there may also be a worry that the excellent progress that they have made will be lost once treatment ends. The end of treatment can also feel like abandonment. This feeling can be particularly challenging for people who are sensitive to perceived rejection. It is therefore not uncommon for symptoms to flare up as we get closer to treatment completion.

However, there are very good reasons why it is important to learn how to say goodbye. For folks who may be relying too much on their therapist, it can be important to develop a sense of self-efficacy in becoming their own therapist. In other cases, the patient simply is no longer profiting from therapy and would benefit from taking some time off therapy or continuing their journey with another clinician. Finally, I think there is an incredible lesson to be learned in being able to say goodbye in a healthy way. Modelling these types of departures in relationships can be a wonderful parting gift for both the patient and the therapist. Just like every beginning has an end, every connection has an eventual goodbye—whether because of treatment completion, physical distance, natural ebbs and flows of relationships, or death—and it is important to still be able to consider these impermanent relationships as meaningful.

But in some ways, in the full spirit of dialectics, I don't think the end of a relationship is truly goodbye. Even if we no longer see each other on a weekly basis, I like to think that we carry a part of every relationship with us throughout our lives. Through these interactions, we have ever so slightly changed each other's lives. I'm very open to sharing these musings with my patients. My patient Avery struggled a lot with feelings of abandonment. During my final treatment session with them, I remember saying that although treatment had to end, I will carry them with me throughout my life. I would continue to occasionally think of them fondly and reminisce about our time with nothing but compassion and loving-kindness. And I hoped that they would do the same for me. Because of their struggles with borderline personality disorder, Avery often felt unstable in many areas of their life. But this was not true of my experience with them. In fact, I thanked Avery for being a great source of stability for me. I told them that I truly appreciated the fact that they rarely missed a treatment session, that they always came to therapy with a willingness to learn, and that they were just generally a good-natured person. The borderline personality disorder clinic was tumultuous in many ways, with rates of patient dropout being quite high, so I was really happy they stuck with me until the end. I think Avery found my self-disclosure regarding my feelings about them to be rather powerful and I hope it modelled how goodbyes can be a positive thing.

I have similar thoughts about all of my patients. I reflect fondly on them and our time together, and I hope that my presence had a small positive impact on their lives. A supervisor once asked me what kind of therapist I aspired to become. I wasn't sure at the time and I'm still not sure now. But I think I might say: "I want to be the kind of therapist that people can say hello and goodbye without fearing the beginning or end of the relationship." I want to be the therapist equivalent of a light breeze—a wind that creates a sense of uplift and calm, helps people stand up a little more confidently, and instills in them a mild sense of wonder and meaning. Yet, no one yearns for the breeze to return. It's a happy meeting with a happy departure. I think this approach is a nice representation of the ethical principles of beneficence and non-maleficence, "doing good" and "doing no harm." I would very much like it if every patient, and in this case every reader, comes out feeling like they got something from the experience, whether it was a small nugget of wisdom or broader reframe in their perspective. Ultimately, it would be nice if the people whose lives I have touched can reflect back to the experience and say this was a good thing.

Finally, I'd like to thank you for taking the time to read this book. Your time is valuable, so I am truly appreciative of your willingness to spend some of that time going through this journey with me. I hope this book was helpful in providing a few tools and a slight reframe in your perspective to better navigate life's challenges. If I have changed your life just a little bit, then I think that is enough. Though maybe we can save the tearful goodbyes for another time. Because who knows, perhaps I'll see you again at some point in our lives. Life can be quite long after all. And of course, you are always welcome to reach out to me. It will be a lovely opportunity to make another connection and another chance to practice a happy goodbye.

Index

Index

www.ingramcontent.com/pod-product-compliance
Lightning Source LLC
LaVergne TN
LVHW010618100826
845148LV00014B/3021
9781476659350